50 Homegrown Harvest Recipes for Home

By: Kelly Johnson

Table of Contents

- Fresh Garden Salad with Herb Vinaigrette
- Heirloom Tomato Bruschetta
- Zucchini Fritters with Yogurt Dill Sauce
- Butternut Squash Soup with Sage
- Roasted Beet and Goat Cheese Salad
- Grilled Corn on the Cob with Chili Lime Butter
- Stuffed Bell Peppers with Quinoa and Chickpeas
- Cucumber Avocado Gazpacho
- Caprese Salad with Balsamic Glaze
- Ratatouille
- Garlic and Herb Roasted Potatoes
- Kale and White Bean Soup
- Pumpkin Risotto with Parmesan
- Fresh Berry Salad with Honey-Lime Dressing
- Eggplant Parmesan
- Cornbread with Maple Butter
- Potato Leek Soup
- Spinach and Feta Stuffed Mushrooms
- Sweet Potato Gnocchi with Brown Butter Sauce
- Green Bean Almondine
- Apple Walnut Salad with Maple Dijon Dressing
- Squash Blossom Quesadillas
- Mushroom and Spinach Stuffed Acorn Squash
- Roasted Brussels Sprouts with Balsamic Glaze
- Strawberry Spinach Salad with Poppy Seed Dressing
- Herb Roasted Carrots
- Stuffed Portobello Mushrooms with Spinach and Cheese
- Lemon Garlic Roasted Broccoli
- Harvest Grain Salad with Citrus Vinaigrette
- Sauteed Swiss Chard with Garlic and Lemon
- Cauliflower Steaks with Chimichurri Sauce
- Asparagus and Gruyere Tart
- Sweet Potato and Black Bean Enchiladas
- Grilled Eggplant with Tahini Sauce
- Beet and Goat Cheese Tartlets
- Parsnip and Apple Soup

- Cherry Tomato and Basil Bruschetta
- Spinach and Ricotta Stuffed Shells
- Roasted Garlic Mashed Potatoes
- Herbed Farro Salad with Roasted Vegetables
- Baked Acorn Squash with Brown Sugar and Cinnamon
- Cabbage Rolls with Tomato Sauce
- Grilled Portobello Mushroom Burgers
- Spring Pea Risotto
- Watermelon and Feta Salad with Mint
- Ratatouille Stuffed Peppers
- Corn and Tomato Pie
- Roasted Cauliflower with Tahini Yogurt Sauce
- Pumpkin and Sage Pasta
- Blueberry Basil Lemonade

Fresh Garden Salad with Herb Vinaigrette

Ingredients:

For the salad:

- Mixed salad greens (lettuce, arugula, spinach, etc.)
- Cherry tomatoes, halved
- Cucumber, thinly sliced
- Red onion, thinly sliced
- Carrot, grated
- Bell peppers, thinly sliced
- Optional: radishes, avocado, or any other vegetables you enjoy

For the Herb Vinaigrette:

- 1/4 cup extra virgin olive oil
- 2 tablespoons red wine vinegar
- 1 tablespoon Dijon mustard
- 1 clove garlic, minced
- 1 teaspoon honey or maple syrup (optional, for sweetness)
- 1 tablespoon fresh herbs, finely chopped (such as parsley, basil, dill, or a mix)
- Salt and pepper to taste

Instructions:

1. **Prepare the Vinaigrette:**
   - In a small bowl, whisk together the olive oil, red wine vinegar, Dijon mustard, minced garlic, and honey or maple syrup (if using).
   - Add the chopped fresh herbs (such as parsley, basil, or dill).
   - Season with salt and pepper to taste. Set aside.
2. **Assemble the Salad:**
   - Wash and dry the mixed salad greens thoroughly.
   - In a large salad bowl, combine the mixed greens, cherry tomatoes, cucumber slices, red onion slices, grated carrot, and bell pepper slices.
   - Add any other vegetables of your choice, such as radishes or avocado.
3. **Serve:**
   - Drizzle the herb vinaigrette over the salad just before serving. Toss gently to coat all the vegetables with the dressing.
   - Serve immediately and enjoy your fresh garden salad!

This salad is versatile and can be customized with your favorite seasonal vegetables and herbs. It's perfect for a light lunch or as a side dish with grilled chicken or fish.

Heirloom Tomato Bruschetta

Ingredients:

- 4-5 medium-sized heirloom tomatoes, diced
- 1-2 cloves garlic, minced
- 1/4 cup fresh basil leaves, thinly sliced
- 2 tablespoons extra virgin olive oil
- 1 tablespoon balsamic vinegar
- Salt and freshly ground black pepper, to taste
- 1 baguette or rustic Italian bread, sliced
- Olive oil, for brushing

Instructions:

1. **Prepare the Tomatoes:**
   - Dice the heirloom tomatoes into small pieces. You can mix different colors and varieties for a visually appealing dish.
2. **Make the Bruschetta Topping:**
   - In a bowl, combine the diced tomatoes, minced garlic, sliced basil leaves, extra virgin olive oil, and balsamic vinegar.
   - Season with salt and pepper to taste. Stir gently to combine all the ingredients. Set aside to marinate for about 15-20 minutes to allow the flavors to meld together.
3. **Prepare the Bread:**
   - Preheat your oven to 375°F (190°C).
   - Slice the baguette or rustic Italian bread into 1/2-inch thick slices. Place the slices on a baking sheet in a single layer.
   - Lightly brush each slice with olive oil on both sides.
4. **Toast the Bread:**
   - Bake the bread slices in the preheated oven for about 8-10 minutes, or until they are crisp and lightly golden brown. You can also toast them on a grill or in a toaster oven.
5. **Assemble the Bruschetta:**
   - Once the bread slices are toasted, remove them from the oven and let them cool slightly.
   - Spoon a generous amount of the tomato mixture onto each toasted bread slice. Make sure to include some of the juices from the tomato mixture.
6. **Serve:**
   - Arrange the Heirloom Tomato Bruschetta on a serving platter.
   - Garnish with additional fresh basil leaves, if desired.
   - Serve immediately and enjoy this delicious appetizer!

Heirloom Tomato Bruschetta is best served fresh, allowing the flavors of the tomatoes and herbs to shine. It's perfect for summer gatherings, parties, or as a starter for a special meal.

Zucchini Fritters with Yogurt Dill Sauce

Ingredients:

For the Zucchini Fritters:

- 2 medium zucchinis (about 1 lb), grated
- 1 teaspoon salt
- 2 green onions, finely chopped
- 1/4 cup fresh dill, chopped
- 1/2 cup grated Parmesan cheese
- 1/2 cup all-purpose flour
- 2 large eggs, lightly beaten
- 1/2 teaspoon baking powder
- Freshly ground black pepper, to taste
- Olive oil, for frying

For the Yogurt Dill Sauce:

- 1 cup Greek yogurt
- 1 tablespoon fresh dill, chopped
- 1 tablespoon lemon juice
- Salt and pepper, to taste

Instructions:

1. **Prepare the Zucchini:**
   - Grate the zucchinis using a box grater or a food processor fitted with a grating attachment.
   - Place the grated zucchini in a colander set over a bowl and sprinkle with salt. Toss to combine and let sit for about 10-15 minutes to draw out excess moisture.
2. **Make the Yogurt Dill Sauce:**
   - In a small bowl, combine the Greek yogurt, chopped dill, lemon juice, salt, and pepper. Mix well and adjust seasoning to taste. Cover and refrigerate until ready to serve.
3. **Prepare the Zucchini Fritters:**
   - After the zucchini has released some moisture, squeeze handfuls of grated zucchini tightly to remove excess liquid. Transfer the squeezed zucchini to a large bowl.
4. **Combine Ingredients:**
   - To the bowl of grated zucchini, add the green onions, chopped dill, grated Parmesan cheese, all-purpose flour, beaten eggs, baking powder, and freshly ground black pepper. Mix well until all ingredients are combined and the mixture holds together.
5. **Cook the Fritters:**

- In a large skillet, heat a thin layer of olive oil over medium-high heat.
- Scoop about 2-3 tablespoons of the zucchini mixture per fritter and carefully drop it into the skillet, flattening slightly with a spatula. Cook for about 3-4 minutes on each side, or until golden brown and crispy. Adjust heat as needed to prevent burning.

6. **Serve:**
    - Transfer the cooked zucchini fritters to a plate lined with paper towels to drain excess oil.
    - Serve the zucchini fritters warm, accompanied by the prepared yogurt dill sauce for dipping or drizzling over the fritters.
    - Garnish with additional fresh dill, if desired.

These Zucchini Fritters with Yogurt Dill Sauce are flavorful, crispy on the outside, and tender on the inside. They make a great appetizer, light lunch, or even a side dish for dinner. Enjoy!

Butternut Squash Soup with Sage

Ingredients:

- 1 medium butternut squash (about 2-3 lbs), peeled, seeded, and diced
- 1 onion, chopped
- 2 cloves garlic, minced
- 4 cups vegetable broth (or chicken broth)
- 1/2 teaspoon ground cinnamon
- 1/4 teaspoon ground nutmeg
- 1/4 teaspoon ground ginger
- Salt and pepper, to taste
- 2 tablespoons olive oil
- 8-10 fresh sage leaves, chopped (plus extra for garnish)
- 1/2 cup heavy cream or coconut cream (optional, for creamier texture)

Instructions:

1. **Prepare the Squash:**
    - Peel the butternut squash using a vegetable peeler. Cut it in half lengthwise, scoop out the seeds with a spoon, and dice the flesh into 1-inch cubes.
2. **Saute the Aromatics:**
    - In a large pot or Dutch oven, heat the olive oil over medium heat. Add the chopped onion and cook until softened and translucent, about 5-7 minutes. Stir occasionally to prevent burning.
    - Add the minced garlic and chopped sage leaves to the pot. Cook for another 1-2 minutes until fragrant.
3. **Cook the Squash:**
    - Add the diced butternut squash to the pot. Season with ground cinnamon, nutmeg, ginger, salt, and pepper. Stir to coat the squash with the spices and aromatics.
    - Pour in the vegetable broth (or chicken broth) until the squash is just covered. Bring the mixture to a boil, then reduce the heat to low and simmer, covered, for about 20-25 minutes, or until the squash is tender and easily pierced with a fork.
4. **Blend the Soup:**
    - Using an immersion blender directly in the pot, blend the soup until smooth and creamy. Alternatively, carefully transfer the soup in batches to a blender and blend until smooth. Be cautious with hot liquids in a blender to avoid splattering.
5. **Finish the Soup:**
    - Stir in the heavy cream or coconut cream (if using) to add a creamy texture and richness to the soup. Taste and adjust seasoning with salt and pepper as needed.
6. **Serve:**

- Ladle the Butternut Squash Soup into bowls. Garnish each serving with a drizzle of cream (if desired), a few chopped sage leaves, and a sprinkle of freshly ground black pepper.
- Serve hot and enjoy this comforting and flavorful Butternut Squash Soup with Sage!

This soup is perfect for cooler weather and makes a satisfying appetizer or light meal served with crusty bread on the side.

Roasted Beet and Goat Cheese Salad

Ingredients:

- 3-4 medium beets, scrubbed and trimmed
- 4 oz goat cheese, crumbled
- 1/4 cup walnuts, toasted and roughly chopped
- Mixed salad greens (such as arugula, spinach, or mixed baby greens)
- Balsamic glaze or reduction, for drizzling (optional)
- Extra virgin olive oil, for roasting and dressing
- Salt and pepper, to taste

Instructions:

1. **Roast the Beets:**
   - Preheat your oven to 400°F (200°C).
   - Wash the beets thoroughly and trim off any stems. Rub each beet with a little olive oil and sprinkle with salt and pepper.
   - Wrap each beet individually in aluminum foil and place them on a baking sheet.
   - Roast in the preheated oven for about 45-60 minutes, or until the beets are tender when pierced with a fork.
   - Once roasted, remove the beets from the oven and let them cool slightly. Use a paper towel to rub off the skin (it should come off easily). Cut the beets into wedges or cubes.
2. **Prepare the Salad:**
   - In a large salad bowl, combine the mixed salad greens with the roasted beet wedges or cubes.
   - Add the crumbled goat cheese and toasted walnuts to the salad.
3. **Make the Dressing:**
   - In a small bowl, whisk together about 2-3 tablespoons of extra virgin olive oil with a pinch of salt and pepper.
   - Optionally, you can drizzle some balsamic glaze or reduction over the salad for added flavor.
4. **Assemble and Serve:**
   - Drizzle the olive oil dressing over the salad and toss gently to combine.
   - Divide the salad among plates or bowls.
   - Optionally, garnish with additional crumbled goat cheese, toasted walnuts, and a drizzle of balsamic glaze.
   - Serve the Roasted Beet and Goat Cheese Salad immediately as a delicious and colorful appetizer or light meal.

This salad combines the earthy sweetness of roasted beets with creamy goat cheese, crunchy walnuts, and fresh greens for a delightful combination of flavors and textures. Enjoy!

Grilled Corn on the Cob with Chili Lime Butter

Ingredients:

- 4 ears of corn, husked
- 4 tablespoons unsalted butter, softened
- Zest of 1 lime
- Juice of 1 lime
- 1 teaspoon chili powder (adjust to taste)
- 1/2 teaspoon ground cumin
- 1/4 teaspoon cayenne pepper (optional, for heat)
- Salt, to taste
- Freshly ground black pepper, to taste
- Chopped fresh cilantro, for garnish (optional)

Instructions:

1. **Prepare the Chili Lime Butter:**
    - In a small bowl, combine the softened butter, lime zest, lime juice, chili powder, ground cumin, cayenne pepper (if using), salt, and black pepper. Mix well until all ingredients are thoroughly combined.
2. **Prepare the Corn:**
    - Preheat your grill to medium-high heat.
    - Husk the corn and remove any silk. Rinse the corn under cold water and pat dry with paper towels.
3. **Grill the Corn:**
    - Place the corn directly on the grill grates. Grill for about 10-12 minutes, turning occasionally, until the corn kernels are tender and lightly charred in spots.
4. **Apply the Chili Lime Butter:**
    - Remove the corn from the grill and immediately brush each ear with the prepared chili lime butter. Make sure to coat each ear evenly with the butter mixture.
5. **Serve:**
    - Transfer the grilled corn on the cob to a serving platter.
    - Garnish with chopped fresh cilantro, if desired.
    - Serve hot and enjoy the delicious flavors of Grilled Corn on the Cob with Chili Lime Butter!

This dish is perfect for summer barbecues or as a side dish for any grilled meal. The combination of zesty lime, spicy chili powder, and creamy butter complements the sweetness of the grilled corn beautifully.

Stuffed Bell Peppers with Quinoa and Chickpeas

Ingredients:

- 4 large bell peppers (any color), tops cut off and seeds removed
- 1 cup quinoa, rinsed
- 1 can (15 oz) chickpeas, drained and rinsed
- 1 cup diced tomatoes (fresh or canned)
- 1/2 cup corn kernels (fresh or frozen)
- 1/2 cup diced onion
- 2 cloves garlic, minced
- 1 teaspoon ground cumin
- 1 teaspoon smoked paprika
- Salt and pepper, to taste
- 1 cup shredded cheese (cheddar, mozzarella, or your choice), divided
- Fresh cilantro or parsley, chopped (for garnish, optional)
- Olive oil, for cooking

Instructions:

1. **Preheat the Oven:**
    - Preheat your oven to 375°F (190°C).
2. **Prepare the Quinoa:**
    - In a medium saucepan, bring 2 cups of water to a boil. Add the rinsed quinoa and a pinch of salt. Reduce the heat to low, cover, and simmer for about 15 minutes, or until the quinoa is cooked and the water is absorbed. Remove from heat and fluff with a fork.
3. **Prepare the Bell Peppers:**
    - Cut the tops off the bell peppers and remove the seeds and membranes. Place the bell peppers upright in a baking dish that's been lightly greased with olive oil.
4. **Make the Filling:**
    - In a large skillet, heat 1-2 tablespoons of olive oil over medium heat. Add the diced onion and cook until softened, about 5 minutes.
    - Add the minced garlic, ground cumin, and smoked paprika to the skillet. Cook for another minute until fragrant.
    - Stir in the diced tomatoes, chickpeas, and corn kernels. Cook for 3-4 minutes until heated through.
    - Add the cooked quinoa to the skillet and stir to combine. Season with salt and pepper to taste. Remove from heat.
    - Stir in 1/2 cup of shredded cheese into the quinoa mixture.
5. **Stuff the Bell Peppers:**
    - Spoon the quinoa and chickpea mixture evenly into each bell pepper until they are filled to the top.
    - Sprinkle the remaining shredded cheese over the tops of the stuffed peppers.
6. **Bake:**

- Cover the baking dish with foil and bake in the preheated oven for 25-30 minutes, or until the bell peppers are tender and the cheese is melted and bubbly.

7. **Serve:**
    - Remove the stuffed bell peppers from the oven and let them cool slightly.
    - Garnish with chopped fresh cilantro or parsley, if desired.
    - Serve hot as a delicious and nutritious main dish.

These Stuffed Bell Peppers with Quinoa and Chickpeas are packed with protein, fiber, and flavor. They make a satisfying vegetarian meal that's perfect for lunch or dinner. Enjoy!

Cucumber Avocado Gazpacho

Ingredients:

- 2 large cucumbers, peeled and chopped
- 1 ripe avocado, peeled and pitted
- 1 green bell pepper, seeded and chopped
- 1/2 small red onion, chopped
- 2 cloves garlic, minced
- 1/4 cup fresh cilantro or parsley, chopped
- 2 tablespoons fresh lime juice
- 1 tablespoon white wine vinegar or apple cider vinegar
- 1 cup cold water or vegetable broth
- Salt and pepper, to taste
- Optional garnishes: diced cucumber, avocado cubes, chopped fresh herbs, drizzle of olive oil

Instructions:

1. **Prepare the Vegetables:**
   - Peel and chop the cucumbers. Reserve about 1/4 cup of diced cucumber for garnish, if desired.
   - Peel and pit the avocado, and chop it roughly.
   - Seed and chop the green bell pepper.
   - Chop the red onion and mince the garlic cloves.
2. **Blend the Soup:**
   - In a blender or food processor, combine the chopped cucumbers, avocado, green bell pepper, red onion, minced garlic, cilantro or parsley, lime juice, and vinegar.
   - Add cold water or vegetable broth to help blend smoothly.
   - Blend until smooth and creamy. You may need to work in batches depending on the size of your blender.
3. **Season and Chill:**
   - Taste the gazpacho and season with salt and pepper to taste. Adjust the acidity with more lime juice or vinegar if needed.
   - Transfer the blended gazpacho to a large bowl or container. Cover and refrigerate for at least 1 hour to chill and allow the flavors to meld together.
4. **Serve:**
   - Stir the chilled gazpacho before serving.
   - Ladle the cucumber avocado gazpacho into bowls or glasses.
   - Garnish with reserved diced cucumber, avocado cubes, chopped fresh herbs, and a drizzle of olive oil, if desired.
   - Serve cold and enjoy this refreshing and creamy soup!

Cucumber Avocado Gazpacho is light, healthy, and packed with nutrients. It's a perfect starter or a refreshing snack on a hot day.

Caprese Salad with Balsamic Glaze

Ingredients:

- 3-4 large ripe tomatoes, sliced
- 1-2 balls of fresh mozzarella cheese, sliced
- Fresh basil leaves
- Balsamic glaze (store-bought or homemade)
- Extra virgin olive oil
- Salt and pepper, to taste

Instructions:

1. **Prepare the Ingredients:**
   - Wash and slice the tomatoes into rounds, about 1/4-inch thick.
   - Slice the fresh mozzarella cheese into similar-sized rounds.
   - Wash and dry the fresh basil leaves.
2. **Assemble the Salad:**
   - On a serving platter or individual plates, arrange the tomato slices, overlapping slightly.
   - Top each tomato slice with a slice of fresh mozzarella cheese.
   - Place a fresh basil leaf on top of each mozzarella slice.
3. **Drizzle with Olive Oil:**
   - Drizzle extra virgin olive oil over the tomato, mozzarella, and basil slices. Use it sparingly, as the flavors are delicate.
4. **Season with Salt and Pepper:**
   - Sprinkle a pinch of salt and freshly ground black pepper over the salad to taste.
5. **Finish with Balsamic Glaze:**
   - Drizzle balsamic glaze over the Caprese salad. Start with a light drizzle and add more according to your preference.
6. **Serve:**
   - Serve the Caprese Salad immediately as a refreshing appetizer or side dish.
   - Optionally, garnish with additional fresh basil leaves for presentation.

Homemade Balsamic Glaze:

- If you'd like to make your own balsamic glaze, here's how:

Ingredients:

- 1 cup balsamic vinegar
- 2 tablespoons honey or brown sugar (optional, for sweetness)

Instructions:

1. In a small saucepan, combine the balsamic vinegar and honey or brown sugar (if using).
2. Bring the mixture to a boil over medium-high heat. Reduce the heat to low and simmer, stirring occasionally, until the vinegar has thickened and reduced by half. This usually takes about 10-15 minutes.
3. Remove from heat and let it cool slightly. The glaze will continue to thicken as it cools.

4. Drizzle the homemade balsamic glaze over your Caprese Salad or store it in a sealed container in the refrigerator for future use.

Enjoy your delicious Caprese Salad with Balsamic Glaze, perfect for showcasing the flavors of summer!

Ratatouille

Ingredients:

- 1 eggplant, diced
- 2 zucchinis, diced
- 1 red bell pepper, diced
- 1 yellow bell pepper, diced
- 1 onion, diced
- 4 cloves garlic, minced
- 4-5 ripe tomatoes, diced (or 1 can of diced tomatoes)
- 2 tablespoons tomato paste
- 2 tablespoons olive oil
- 1 teaspoon dried thyme
- 1 teaspoon dried oregano
- Salt and pepper, to taste
- Fresh basil or parsley, chopped (for garnish)

Instructions:

1. **Prepare the Vegetables:**
   - Dice the eggplant, zucchinis, red bell pepper, yellow bell pepper, and onion into evenly sized pieces.
2. **Cook the Vegetables:**
   - In a large skillet or Dutch oven, heat the olive oil over medium heat.
   - Add the diced onion and cook until softened, about 5 minutes.
   - Add the minced garlic and cook for another minute until fragrant.
3. **Add Tomatoes and Tomato Paste:**
   - Stir in the diced tomatoes and tomato paste. Cook for 5-7 minutes, stirring occasionally, until the tomatoes start to break down and release their juices.
4. **Add Remaining Vegetables:**
   - Add the diced eggplant, zucchinis, red bell pepper, and yellow bell pepper to the skillet.
   - Season with dried thyme, dried oregano, salt, and pepper to taste. Stir well to combine all ingredients.
5. **Simmer:**
   - Reduce the heat to low and cover the skillet or Dutch oven. Let the ratatouille simmer for about 30-40 minutes, stirring occasionally, until the vegetables are tender and the flavors have melded together. If the mixture becomes too dry, add a splash of water or vegetable broth.
6. **Serve:**
   - Once cooked, taste and adjust seasoning if needed.
   - Garnish with chopped fresh basil or parsley before serving.
7. **Enjoy:**
   - Serve Ratatouille warm or at room temperature as a side dish, over pasta or rice, or even as a main dish with crusty bread.

Ratatouille is a versatile dish that can be enjoyed freshly made or even as leftovers, as the flavors continue to develop over time. It's a delicious way to enjoy a variety of seasonal vegetables in one comforting dish.

Garlic and Herb Roasted Potatoes

Ingredients:

- 1.5 lbs (about 680g) baby potatoes, halved or quartered if large
- 3-4 cloves garlic, minced
- 2-3 tablespoons olive oil
- 1 teaspoon dried thyme
- 1 teaspoon dried rosemary
- 1/2 teaspoon dried oregano
- Salt and pepper, to taste
- Fresh parsley, chopped (for garnish, optional)

Instructions:

1. **Preheat the Oven:**
   - Preheat your oven to 400°F (200°C).
2. **Prepare the Potatoes:**
   - Wash and scrub the baby potatoes thoroughly. If they are large, halve or quarter them to ensure even cooking.
3. **Season the Potatoes:**
   - In a large bowl, toss the potatoes with minced garlic, olive oil, dried thyme, dried rosemary, dried oregano, salt, and pepper. Make sure the potatoes are evenly coated with the oil and herbs.
4. **Roast the Potatoes:**
   - Spread the seasoned potatoes in a single layer on a baking sheet lined with parchment paper or aluminum foil.
   - Roast in the preheated oven for 30-35 minutes, or until the potatoes are golden brown and tender, stirring once halfway through cooking to ensure even browning.
5. **Serve:**
   - Remove the roasted potatoes from the oven and transfer them to a serving dish.
   - Garnish with freshly chopped parsley, if desired, before serving.

Garlic and Herb Roasted Potatoes are a versatile side dish that pairs well with chicken, beef, fish, or even as part of a vegetarian meal. They are crispy on the outside, tender on the inside, and packed with delicious flavors from the garlic and herbs. Enjoy!

Kale and White Bean Soup

Ingredients:

- 1 tablespoon olive oil
- 1 onion, chopped
- 2 carrots, diced
- 2 celery stalks, diced
- 3 cloves garlic, minced
- 1 teaspoon dried thyme
- 1 teaspoon dried rosemary
- 1 bay leaf
- 4 cups vegetable broth or chicken broth
- 2 (15 oz) cans white beans (such as cannellini or navy beans), drained and rinsed
- 1 bunch kale, stems removed and leaves chopped
- Salt and pepper, to taste
- Fresh lemon juice, to taste (optional)
- Grated Parmesan cheese, for serving (optional)

Instructions:

1. **Saute the Vegetables:**
    - In a large pot or Dutch oven, heat olive oil over medium heat. Add chopped onion, diced carrots, and diced celery. Cook, stirring occasionally, until vegetables are softened, about 5-7 minutes.
2. **Add Garlic and Herbs:**
    - Add minced garlic, dried thyme, dried rosemary, and bay leaf to the pot. Cook for 1-2 minutes until fragrant.
3. **Add Broth and Beans:**
    - Pour in vegetable broth or chicken broth, and add drained and rinsed white beans. Bring to a boil.
4. **Simmer:**
    - Reduce heat to low, cover, and simmer for 15-20 minutes to allow flavors to meld together.
5. **Add Kale:**
    - Stir in chopped kale leaves into the soup. Cook for an additional 5-10 minutes, until kale is wilted and tender.
6. **Season and Serve:**
    - Remove bay leaf from the soup. Taste and adjust seasoning with salt and pepper as needed.
    - If desired, add a squeeze of fresh lemon juice to brighten the flavors.
7. **Serve Hot:**
    - Ladle the kale and white bean soup into bowls. Optionally, garnish with grated Parmesan cheese before serving.

This Kale and White Bean Soup is comforting, packed with fiber and protein from the beans, and loaded with vitamins from the kale. It's perfect as a main dish or served with crusty bread for a satisfying meal. Enjoy!

Pumpkin Risotto with Parmesan

Ingredients:

- 1 cup Arborio rice
- 1 small onion, finely chopped
- 2 cloves garlic, minced
- 1 cup canned pumpkin puree
- 4 cups vegetable broth, kept warm
- 1/2 cup dry white wine (optional)
- 1/2 cup grated Parmesan cheese
- 2 tablespoons unsalted butter
- 1 tablespoon olive oil
- 1/2 teaspoon ground nutmeg
- Salt and pepper, to taste
- Fresh parsley, chopped (for garnish)

Instructions:

1. **Prepare the Broth:**
    - In a saucepan, heat the vegetable broth over low heat and keep it warm.
2. **Saute the Onion and Garlic:**
    - In a large, deep skillet or pot, heat the olive oil and butter over medium heat.
    - Add the finely chopped onion and cook until softened, about 3-4 minutes.
    - Add the minced garlic and cook for another 1-2 minutes until fragrant.
3. **Toast the Rice:**
    - Add the Arborio rice to the skillet with the onion and garlic. Stir well to coat the rice with the oil and butter. Toast the rice for 1-2 minutes until lightly golden.
4. **Add Pumpkin and Wine:**
    - Stir in the pumpkin puree and ground nutmeg, mixing well with the rice mixture.
    - If using, pour in the white wine and stir until it's absorbed by the rice.
5. **Cook the Risotto:**
    - Begin adding the warm vegetable broth to the rice mixture, one ladleful at a time. Stir constantly and allow each ladleful of broth to be absorbed before adding the next. This process will take about 20-25 minutes. The rice should be creamy and tender, with a slight bite (al dente).
6. **Finish the Risotto:**
    - Once the rice is cooked to your desired consistency, remove the skillet from heat.
    - Stir in the grated Parmesan cheese until melted and well combined. Season with salt and pepper to taste.
7. **Serve:**
    - Spoon the Pumpkin Risotto into serving bowls.
    - Garnish with chopped fresh parsley and an extra sprinkle of Parmesan cheese, if desired.
    - Serve hot and enjoy this creamy and comforting Pumpkin Risotto with Parmesan!

This dish is rich in flavor and makes a wonderful main course or side dish during the fall season. Pair it with a crisp green salad and a glass of white wine for a complete meal.

Fresh Berry Salad with Honey-Lime Dressing

Ingredients:

- 4 cups mixed fresh berries (such as strawberries, blueberries, raspberries, blackberries)
- 1 tablespoon honey
- Juice of 1 lime
- Zest of 1 lime
- Fresh mint leaves, chopped (optional, for garnish)

Instructions:

1. **Prepare the Berries:**
    - Wash the berries thoroughly and pat them dry with paper towels. If using strawberries, hull and slice them.
2. **Make the Honey-Lime Dressing:**
    - In a small bowl, whisk together the honey, lime juice, and lime zest until well combined. Adjust the sweetness to your taste by adding more honey if desired.
3. **Assemble the Salad:**
    - Place the mixed fresh berries in a large serving bowl or individual serving dishes.
4. **Drizzle with Dressing:**
    - Drizzle the honey-lime dressing over the berries.
5. **Garnish:**
    - Optionally, garnish the salad with chopped fresh mint leaves for an extra burst of freshness.
6. **Serve:**
    - Serve the Fresh Berry Salad immediately as a light and healthy dessert or side dish.

This Fresh Berry Salad with Honey-Lime Dressing is vibrant, colorful, and bursting with natural sweetness. It's a perfect dish to enjoy during hot summer days or as a refreshing conclusion to any meal. Adjust the types of berries based on what's in season for the best flavor.

Eggplant Parmesan

Ingredients:

- 2 medium eggplants, sliced into 1/2-inch rounds
- Salt, for sprinkling
- 1 cup all-purpose flour
- 3 large eggs, beaten
- 2 cups breadcrumbs (preferably Italian-style)
- 1 cup grated Parmesan cheese
- 2 cups marinara sauce (store-bought or homemade)
- 1 cup shredded mozzarella cheese
- 1/2 cup shredded Parmesan cheese
- Fresh basil or parsley, chopped (for garnish)

Instructions:

1. **Preheat the Oven:**
    - Preheat your oven to 375°F (190°C). Lightly grease a large baking dish with olive oil or cooking spray.
2. **Prepare the Eggplant:**
    - Place the eggplant slices in a single layer on a baking sheet lined with paper towels. Sprinkle salt over both sides of each slice. Let them sit for about 30 minutes to release excess moisture. Pat dry with paper towels.
3. **Breading the Eggplant:**
    - Set up a breading station with three shallow dishes: one with flour, one with beaten eggs, and one with breadcrumbs mixed with grated Parmesan cheese.
    - Dredge each eggplant slice in flour, shaking off any excess.
    - Dip in the beaten eggs, allowing any excess to drip off.
    - Coat evenly with the breadcrumb and Parmesan mixture, pressing gently to adhere. Repeat with all eggplant slices.
4. **Frying the Eggplant (Optional):**
    - Heat about 1/4 inch of olive oil in a large skillet over medium-high heat. Fry the breaded eggplant slices in batches until golden brown on both sides, about 2-3 minutes per side. Transfer to a paper towel-lined plate to drain excess oil.
5. **Assembling the Eggplant Parmesan:**
    - Spread a thin layer of marinara sauce on the bottom of the prepared baking dish.
    - Arrange a single layer of fried (or unbaked, if skipping frying step) eggplant slices over the sauce.
    - Spoon marinara sauce over each eggplant slice, followed by a sprinkle of shredded mozzarella and Parmesan cheeses.
    - Repeat the layers (eggplant, sauce, cheeses) until all ingredients are used, finishing with a layer of sauce and cheeses on top.
6. **Baking:**

- Cover the baking dish with aluminum foil and bake in the preheated oven for 30 minutes.
- Remove the foil and bake for an additional 10-15 minutes, or until the cheese is melted and bubbly and the eggplant is tender.

7. **Serve:**
   - Let the Eggplant Parmesan cool slightly before serving.
   - Garnish with chopped fresh basil or parsley.

Eggplant Parmesan is best served warm, accompanied by a side of pasta or a crisp green salad. It's a comforting and satisfying dish that showcases the flavors of eggplant and Italian cheeses beautifully. Enjoy!

Cornbread with Maple Butter

Ingredients:

For the Cornbread:

- 1 cup cornmeal
- 1 cup all-purpose flour
- 1/4 cup granulated sugar
- 1 tablespoon baking powder
- 1/2 teaspoon baking soda
- 1/2 teaspoon salt
- 1 cup buttermilk
- 1/2 cup unsalted butter, melted and cooled slightly
- 2 large eggs

For the Maple Butter:

- 1/2 cup unsalted butter, softened
- 2-3 tablespoons pure maple syrup (adjust to taste)

Instructions:

1. **Preheat the Oven:**
   - Preheat your oven to 375°F (190°C). Grease a 9-inch square baking dish or a cast iron skillet with butter or cooking spray.
2. **Make the Cornbread:**
   - In a large bowl, whisk together the cornmeal, flour, sugar, baking powder, baking soda, and salt.
3. **Combine Wet Ingredients:**
   - In another bowl, whisk together the buttermilk, melted butter, and eggs until well combined.
4. **Mix Batter:**
   - Pour the wet ingredients into the dry ingredients. Stir gently until just combined. Do not overmix; a few lumps are okay.
5. **Bake:**
   - Pour the batter into the prepared baking dish or skillet, spreading it evenly.
   - Bake in the preheated oven for 20-25 minutes, or until the cornbread is golden brown and a toothpick inserted into the center comes out clean.
6. **Make Maple Butter:**
   - While the cornbread is baking, prepare the maple butter by combining softened butter and maple syrup in a small bowl. Mix until smooth and well combined.
7. **Serve:**
   - Remove the cornbread from the oven and let it cool for a few minutes in the baking dish or skillet.

- Serve slices of warm cornbread with a dollop of maple butter on top.

Cornbread with Maple Butter is a comforting treat that balances the savory cornbread with the sweet and slightly tangy maple butter. It's perfect for breakfast, brunch, or as a side dish with chili or barbecue meals. Enjoy the delicious flavors!

Potato Leek Soup

Ingredients:

- 3-4 leeks, white and light green parts only, sliced
- 3-4 medium potatoes, peeled and diced
- 1 onion, chopped
- 2 cloves garlic, minced
- 4 cups vegetable or chicken broth
- 1 cup milk or cream (or use more broth for a lighter version)
- 2 tablespoons butter or olive oil
- Salt and pepper, to taste
- Fresh thyme or parsley, chopped (for garnish, optional)

Instructions:

1. **Prepare the Leeks:**
    - Trim off the root ends and tough dark green parts of the leeks. Slice the leeks lengthwise and then crosswise into half-moons. Rinse thoroughly under cold water to remove any grit.
2. **Saute the Vegetables:**
    - In a large pot or Dutch oven, heat the butter or olive oil over medium heat. Add the chopped onion and cook until translucent, about 5 minutes.
    - Add the sliced leeks and minced garlic. Cook, stirring occasionally, until the leeks are softened, about 5-7 minutes.
3. **Add Potatoes and Broth:**
    - Add the diced potatoes to the pot. Pour in the vegetable or chicken broth. Bring to a boil, then reduce the heat to low and simmer, covered, for about 15-20 minutes, or until the potatoes are tender and easily pierced with a fork.
4. **Blend the Soup (Optional):**
    - For a smoother texture, use an immersion blender to puree the soup directly in the pot until desired consistency is reached. Alternatively, transfer half of the soup to a blender and blend until smooth, then return to the pot.
5. **Add Milk or Cream:**
    - Stir in the milk or cream (or additional broth, if preferred) into the soup. Heat gently over low heat until warmed through, but do not boil.
6. **Season and Serve:**
    - Season with salt and pepper to taste.
    - Ladle the Potato Leek Soup into bowls. Garnish with chopped fresh thyme or parsley, if desired.
7. **Serve Hot:**
    - Serve the soup hot, accompanied by crusty bread or a side salad.

This Potato Leek Soup is creamy, comforting, and packed with flavor from the leeks and potatoes. It's a perfect dish for lunch or dinner, especially during colder seasons. Enjoy the hearty goodness of this classic soup!

Spinach and Feta Stuffed Mushrooms

Ingredients:

- 16 large white mushrooms, stems removed and reserved
- 2 cups fresh spinach, chopped
- 1/2 cup crumbled feta cheese
- 1/4 cup grated Parmesan cheese
- 2 cloves garlic, minced
- 1/4 cup breadcrumbs
- 2 tablespoons olive oil
- Salt and pepper, to taste
- Fresh parsley, chopped (for garnish)

Instructions:

1. **Prepare the Mushrooms:**
    - Preheat your oven to 375°F (190°C). Line a baking sheet with parchment paper or lightly grease it.
    - Remove the stems from the mushrooms and finely chop them. Set the mushroom caps aside.
2. **Make the Filling:**
    - Heat olive oil in a large skillet over medium heat. Add the chopped mushroom stems and minced garlic. Cook for 3-4 minutes until softened.
    - Add the chopped spinach to the skillet and cook for another 2-3 minutes until wilted. Season with salt and pepper to taste.
3. **Assemble the Stuffing:**
    - Remove the skillet from heat. Stir in the crumbled feta cheese, grated Parmesan cheese, and breadcrumbs. Mix well until combined.
4. **Stuff the Mushrooms:**
    - Spoon the spinach and feta mixture into the mushroom caps, filling each one generously.
5. **Bake the Stuffed Mushrooms:**
    - Place the stuffed mushrooms on the prepared baking sheet. Bake in the preheated oven for 15-20 minutes, or until the mushrooms are tender and the filling is golden brown.
6. **Serve:**
    - Remove from the oven and let cool slightly. Garnish with chopped fresh parsley before serving.

Spinach and Feta Stuffed Mushrooms are flavorful and savory, with the earthy taste of mushrooms complementing the creamy spinach and tangy feta cheese filling. They make an impressive appetizer for parties or a tasty side dish for any meal. Enjoy!

Sweet Potato Gnocchi with Brown Butter Sauce

Ingredients:

For the Sweet Potato Gnocchi:

- 2 medium sweet potatoes (about 1 lb total)
- 1 cup ricotta cheese
- 1 egg, lightly beaten
- 1 teaspoon salt
- 1/4 teaspoon ground nutmeg
- 2-3 cups all-purpose flour, plus more for dusting

For the Brown Butter Sauce:

- 1/2 cup unsalted butter
- 2 cloves garlic, minced
- Fresh sage leaves (about 8-10 leaves), chopped
- Salt and pepper, to taste
- Grated Parmesan cheese, for serving (optional)

Instructions:

1. **Prepare the Sweet Potatoes:**
   - Preheat your oven to 400°F (200°C). Pierce the sweet potatoes with a fork in several places and place them on a baking sheet.
   - Bake for 45-60 minutes, or until tender. Remove from the oven and let cool slightly.
2. **Make the Sweet Potato Gnocchi:**
   - Scoop the flesh from the sweet potatoes into a large mixing bowl. Mash the sweet potatoes until smooth.
   - Add the ricotta cheese, beaten egg, salt, and ground nutmeg to the bowl. Mix well to combine.
   - Gradually add 2 cups of flour, mixing with a wooden spoon or your hands until the dough comes together and is slightly sticky. Add more flour as needed, a little at a time, until the dough is soft and pliable but not sticky.
3. **Form the Gnocchi:**
   - On a lightly floured surface, divide the dough into several portions. Roll each portion into a long rope about 1/2 inch thick. Cut the rope into 1-inch pieces.
4. **Shape the Gnocchi:**
   - Optional: Roll each piece of dough over the tines of a fork to create ridges (this helps sauce adhere better).
   - Place the shaped gnocchi on a floured baking sheet or tray.
5. **Cook the Gnocchi:**

- Bring a large pot of salted water to a boil. Working in batches, carefully drop the gnocchi into the boiling water. Cook until they float to the surface, about 2-3 minutes. Remove with a slotted spoon and transfer to a plate.

6. **Make the Brown Butter Sauce:**
    - In a large skillet, melt the butter over medium heat. Cook, stirring occasionally, until the butter turns a light golden brown color and gives off a nutty aroma, about 3-5 minutes.
    - Add the minced garlic and chopped sage leaves to the brown butter. Cook for another 1-2 minutes, stirring constantly, until the garlic is fragrant and the sage leaves are crispy. Season with salt and pepper to taste.

7. **Serve:**
    - Add the cooked gnocchi to the skillet with the brown butter sauce. Gently toss to coat the gnocchi evenly with the sauce.
    - Serve the Sweet Potato Gnocchi with Brown Butter Sauce immediately, garnished with grated Parmesan cheese if desired.

Sweet Potato Gnocchi with Brown Butter Sauce is a delightful dish that combines soft, pillowy gnocchi with a rich and flavorful sauce. It's perfect for a cozy dinner or a special occasion. Enjoy the sweet and savory flavors!

Green Bean Almondine

Ingredients:

- 1 lb (450g) fresh green beans, trimmed
- 1/2 cup sliced almonds
- 4 tablespoons unsalted butter
- 2 tablespoons fresh lemon juice
- Zest of 1 lemon
- Salt and pepper, to taste
- Fresh parsley, chopped (optional, for garnish)

Instructions:

1. **Blanch the Green Beans:**
    - Bring a large pot of salted water to a boil. Add the trimmed green beans and cook for 3-4 minutes, or until they are bright green and crisp-tender. Drain the beans and immediately plunge them into a bowl of ice water to stop the cooking process. Drain again and set aside.
2. **Toast the Almonds:**
    - In a large skillet, toast the sliced almonds over medium heat until they are golden and fragrant, about 3-4 minutes. Stir frequently to prevent burning. Transfer the toasted almonds to a plate and set aside.
3. **Make the Brown Butter Sauce:**
    - In the same skillet, melt the butter over medium heat. Continue to cook the butter, swirling the pan occasionally, until it turns a light golden brown color and gives off a nutty aroma, about 3-4 minutes.
4. **Combine the Ingredients:**
    - Add the blanched green beans to the skillet with the brown butter sauce. Toss gently to coat the beans evenly with the butter.
    - Stir in the fresh lemon juice and lemon zest. Season with salt and pepper to taste.
5. **Serve:**
    - Transfer the Green Bean Almondine to a serving dish.
    - Sprinkle the toasted almonds over the top.
    - Optionally, garnish with chopped fresh parsley for color and extra flavor.

Green Bean Almondine is best served warm as a side dish to complement roasted meats, fish, or as part of a vegetarian meal. The combination of tender green beans, crunchy almonds, and tangy lemon butter sauce makes it a delightful addition to any dinner table. Enjoy!

Apple Walnut Salad with Maple Dijon Dressing

Ingredients:

For the Salad:

- 6 cups mixed salad greens (such as baby spinach, arugula, or mixed greens)
- 2 apples, cored and thinly sliced (use your favorite variety)
- 1/2 cup walnuts, toasted and chopped
- 1/4 cup dried cranberries or raisins (optional)
- 1/4 cup crumbled feta or goat cheese (optional)

For the Maple Dijon Dressing:

- 1/4 cup olive oil
- 2 tablespoons apple cider vinegar or white wine vinegar
- 1 tablespoon maple syrup
- 1 tablespoon Dijon mustard
- Salt and pepper, to taste

Instructions:

1. **Prepare the Salad Greens:**
    - In a large salad bowl, toss together the mixed salad greens.
2. **Add Apples and Walnuts:**
    - Arrange the thinly sliced apples over the salad greens. Sprinkle with toasted and chopped walnuts. Add dried cranberries or raisins and crumbled feta or goat cheese, if using.
3. **Make the Maple Dijon Dressing:**
    - In a small bowl or jar, whisk together the olive oil, apple cider vinegar, maple syrup, Dijon mustard, salt, and pepper until well combined.
4. **Dress the Salad:**
    - Drizzle the Maple Dijon Dressing over the salad just before serving. Toss gently to coat the salad ingredients evenly with the dressing.
5. **Serve:**
    - Transfer the Apple Walnut Salad with Maple Dijon Dressing to serving plates or bowls.
    - Optionally, garnish with additional walnuts or crumbled cheese on top.
    - Serve immediately and enjoy!

This Apple Walnut Salad with Maple Dijon Dressing is perfect as a light lunch or as a refreshing side dish for dinner. The combination of sweet apples, crunchy walnuts, and the tangy-sweet dressing creates a harmonious blend of flavors and textures. It's also versatile—feel free to customize it with your favorite salad ingredients or protein toppings.

Squash Blossom Quesadillas

Ingredients:

- 8-10 squash blossoms, cleaned and stems removed
- 4 large flour tortillas (10-inch diameter)
- 1 cup shredded Oaxaca cheese or mozzarella cheese
- 1 cup shredded Monterey Jack cheese
- 1/2 cup crumbled queso fresco or feta cheese
- 1 tablespoon olive oil or vegetable oil
- Salt and pepper, to taste
- Salsa, guacamole, or sour cream, for serving (optional)

Instructions:

1. **Prepare the Squash Blossoms:**
    - Gently rinse the squash blossoms under cold water to remove any dirt or insects. Carefully pat them dry with paper towels. Remove the stems and discard.
2. **Assemble the Quesadillas:**
    - Lay out 2 tortillas on a clean surface. Divide the shredded Oaxaca or mozzarella cheese, Monterey Jack cheese, and crumbled queso fresco evenly over the tortillas, leaving a small border around the edges.
3. **Add Squash Blossoms:**
    - Arrange the cleaned squash blossoms evenly over the cheese on each tortilla. Sprinkle with salt and pepper to taste.
4. **Top with More Cheese:**
    - Sprinkle another layer of shredded cheese over the squash blossoms.
5. **Cover with Another Tortilla:**
    - Place the remaining 2 tortillas on top of each filled tortilla to create 2 quesadilla sandwiches.
6. **Cook the Quesadillas:**
    - Heat a large skillet or griddle over medium heat. Brush lightly with olive oil or vegetable oil.
    - Carefully transfer one quesadilla to the skillet. Cook for 3-4 minutes on each side, or until the tortilla is golden brown and the cheese is melted and gooey. Press down gently with a spatula while cooking to ensure even melting.
7. **Serve:**
    - Remove the cooked quesadillas from the skillet and let them rest for a minute before slicing into wedges.
    - Serve the Squash Blossom Quesadillas warm, with salsa, guacamole, or sour cream on the side if desired.

Squash Blossom Quesadillas are a delicious and unique dish that showcases the delicate flavor of squash blossoms. They are perfect as an appetizer, light lunch, or even a vegetarian dinner option. Enjoy the creamy cheese and tender squash blossoms wrapped in warm, crispy tortillas!

Mushroom and Spinach Stuffed Acorn Squash

Ingredients:

- 2 acorn squash
- 2 tablespoons olive oil, divided
- Salt and pepper, to taste
- 1 onion, diced
- 2 cloves garlic, minced
- 8 oz (225g) mushrooms, chopped (such as cremini or button mushrooms)
- 4 cups fresh spinach leaves
- 1/2 cup cooked quinoa or rice (optional, for added texture)
- 1/4 cup grated Parmesan cheese (optional)
- 1/4 teaspoon dried thyme
- 1/4 teaspoon dried sage
- Pinch of red pepper flakes (optional)
- 1/4 cup chopped walnuts or pecans (optional, for garnish)
- Fresh parsley, chopped (for garnish)

Instructions:

1. **Preheat the Oven:**
    - Preheat your oven to 400°F (200°C).
2. **Prepare the Acorn Squash:**
    - Cut the acorn squash in half lengthwise and scoop out the seeds and stringy pulp with a spoon. Brush the cut sides of the squash halves with 1 tablespoon of olive oil and sprinkle with salt and pepper.
    - Place the squash halves cut-side down on a baking sheet lined with parchment paper. Bake for 30-40 minutes, or until the squash is tender when pierced with a fork.
3. **Prepare the Filling:**
    - While the squash is baking, heat the remaining 1 tablespoon of olive oil in a large skillet over medium heat. Add the diced onion and cook for 3-4 minutes until softened.
    - Add the minced garlic and cook for another 1-2 minutes until fragrant.
    - Add the chopped mushrooms to the skillet and cook for 5-6 minutes until they release their moisture and start to brown.
4. **Add Spinach and Seasonings:**
    - Add the fresh spinach leaves to the skillet. Cook, stirring, until the spinach is wilted.
    - Stir in the cooked quinoa or rice (if using), grated Parmesan cheese (if using), dried thyme, dried sage, and a pinch of red pepper flakes. Season with salt and pepper to taste. Cook for another 2-3 minutes to blend the flavors.
5. **Stuff the Acorn Squash:**

- Once the squash halves are tender, remove them from the oven and flip them over so the cut sides are facing up.
- Divide the mushroom and spinach filling evenly among the squash halves, packing it gently into each cavity.

6. **Finish and Serve:**
    - Return the stuffed acorn squash to the oven and bake for an additional 10-15 minutes, or until heated through and slightly golden on top.
    - Remove from the oven and let cool for a few minutes before serving.
    - Garnish with chopped walnuts or pecans and fresh parsley before serving, if desired.

Mushroom and Spinach Stuffed Acorn Squash is a wholesome and satisfying dish that makes a perfect main course for a vegetarian meal or a flavorful side dish. Enjoy the combination of tender squash, savory mushrooms, and nutritious spinach in every bite!

Roasted Brussels Sprouts with Balsamic Glaze

Ingredients:

- 1 lb (450g) Brussels sprouts, trimmed and halved
- 2 tablespoons olive oil
- Salt and pepper, to taste
- 2-3 tablespoons balsamic glaze (store-bought or homemade*)

Instructions:

1. **Preheat the Oven:**
   - Preheat your oven to 400°F (200°C).
2. **Prepare the Brussels Sprouts:**
   - Trim the ends of the Brussels sprouts and cut them in half lengthwise. Remove any outer leaves that are loose or discolored.
3. **Roast the Brussels Sprouts:**
   - Place the halved Brussels sprouts on a large baking sheet. Drizzle with olive oil and season with salt and pepper. Toss well to coat the Brussels sprouts evenly.
4. **Roast in the Oven:**
   - Spread the Brussels sprouts out in a single layer on the baking sheet. Roast in the preheated oven for 20-25 minutes, stirring halfway through, until they are tender and lightly caramelized.
5. **Add the Balsamic Glaze:**
   - Remove the Brussels sprouts from the oven and drizzle with balsamic glaze while they are still warm. Toss gently to coat the Brussels sprouts with the glaze.
6. **Serve:**
   - Transfer the roasted Brussels sprouts to a serving dish. Optionally, drizzle with a bit more balsamic glaze for extra flavor.
   - Serve immediately as a delicious and flavorful side dish.

- **Homemade Balsamic Glaze:**
  - To make your own balsamic glaze, simply simmer balsamic vinegar in a small saucepan over medium heat until it reduces by half and becomes thick and syrupy. Allow it to cool before using.

Roasted Brussels Sprouts with Balsamic Glaze are perfect alongside roasted meats, grilled chicken, or as part of a vegetarian meal. They bring out the best flavors of Brussels sprouts, with the added richness and depth from the balsamic glaze. Enjoy this simple yet elegant dish!

Strawberry Spinach Salad with Poppy Seed Dressing

Ingredients:

For the Salad:

- 6 cups baby spinach leaves, washed and dried
- 1 pint (about 2 cups) fresh strawberries, hulled and sliced
- 1/2 cup sliced almonds, toasted
- 1/4 cup red onion, thinly sliced (optional)
- 1/4 cup crumbled feta cheese or goat cheese (optional)

For the Poppy Seed Dressing:

- 1/3 cup olive oil
- 3 tablespoons apple cider vinegar or white wine vinegar
- 2 tablespoons honey or maple syrup
- 1 tablespoon Dijon mustard
- 1 tablespoon poppy seeds
- Salt and pepper, to taste

Instructions:

1. **Prepare the Salad:**
   - In a large salad bowl, combine the baby spinach leaves, sliced strawberries, toasted sliced almonds, red onion (if using), and crumbled feta or goat cheese (if using).
2. **Make the Poppy Seed Dressing:**
   - In a small bowl or jar, whisk together the olive oil, apple cider vinegar or white wine vinegar, honey or maple syrup, Dijon mustard, poppy seeds, salt, and pepper until well combined.
3. **Assemble the Salad:**
   - Drizzle the poppy seed dressing over the salad ingredients. Toss gently to coat the salad evenly with the dressing.
4. **Serve:**
   - Transfer the Strawberry Spinach Salad to serving plates or bowls.
   - Optionally, garnish with additional sliced strawberries, almonds, or crumbled cheese on top.
   - Serve immediately and enjoy the fresh and vibrant flavors!

This Strawberry Spinach Salad with Poppy Seed Dressing is perfect as a light lunch or as a refreshing side dish for dinner. The combination of sweet strawberries, crunchy almonds, and the tangy-sweet dressing creates a delicious and satisfying salad. It's also versatile—feel free to customize it with your favorite salad ingredients or protein toppings.

Herb Roasted Carrots

Ingredients:

- 1 lb (450g) carrots, peeled and trimmed
- 2 tablespoons olive oil
- 2 cloves garlic, minced
- 1 tablespoon chopped fresh herbs (such as rosemary, thyme, or parsley)
- Salt and pepper, to taste

Instructions:

1. **Preheat the Oven:**
    - Preheat your oven to 400°F (200°C).
2. **Prepare the Carrots:**
    - Peel the carrots and trim off the ends. If the carrots are thick, you can slice them lengthwise into halves or quarters for even cooking.
3. **Season the Carrots:**
    - In a large bowl, toss the carrots with olive oil, minced garlic, chopped fresh herbs, salt, and pepper until evenly coated.
4. **Roast the Carrots:**
    - Arrange the seasoned carrots in a single layer on a baking sheet lined with parchment paper or aluminum foil.
5. **Bake in the Oven:**
    - Roast the carrots in the preheated oven for 20-25 minutes, or until they are tender and lightly caramelized. Stir or flip halfway through cooking to ensure even roasting.
6. **Serve:**
    - Remove the roasted carrots from the oven and transfer them to a serving dish.
    - Garnish with additional chopped fresh herbs if desired.
    - Serve hot as a delicious side dish alongside your favorite main course.

Herb Roasted Carrots are a versatile side dish that pairs well with chicken, beef, pork, or fish. The combination of garlic, herbs, and olive oil brings out the natural sweetness of the carrots, making them a flavorful addition to any meal. Enjoy the delicious and nutritious roasted carrots!

Stuffed Portobello Mushrooms with Spinach and Cheese

Ingredients:

- 4 large portobello mushrooms, stems removed and cleaned
- 2 tablespoons olive oil
- 2 cloves garlic, minced
- 4 cups fresh spinach leaves, chopped
- 1/2 cup ricotta cheese
- 1/2 cup shredded mozzarella cheese
- 1/4 cup grated Parmesan cheese
- 1/4 teaspoon red pepper flakes (optional, for a bit of heat)
- Salt and pepper, to taste
- Fresh parsley, chopped (for garnish)

Instructions:

1. **Preheat the Oven:**
   - Preheat your oven to 375°F (190°C).
2. **Prepare the Portobello Mushrooms:**
   - Remove the stems from the portobello mushrooms and gently scrape out the gills using a spoon. Place the mushrooms on a baking sheet lined with parchment paper.
3. **Prepare the Filling:**
   - In a large skillet, heat olive oil over medium heat. Add minced garlic and cook for 1-2 minutes until fragrant.
   - Add chopped spinach to the skillet and cook until wilted, about 3-4 minutes. Season with salt and pepper to taste.
4. **Make the Cheese Filling:**
   - In a mixing bowl, combine ricotta cheese, shredded mozzarella cheese, grated Parmesan cheese, and red pepper flakes (if using). Add the cooked spinach mixture and stir until well combined.
5. **Stuff the Mushrooms:**
   - Divide the cheese and spinach mixture evenly among the portobello mushroom caps, pressing the mixture gently into each mushroom.
6. **Bake the Stuffed Mushrooms:**
   - Bake in the preheated oven for 20-25 minutes, or until the mushrooms are tender and the cheese is melted and bubbly.
7. **Serve:**
   - Remove the stuffed portobello mushrooms from the oven and let them cool slightly.
   - Garnish with chopped fresh parsley before serving.

Stuffed Portobello Mushrooms with Spinach and Cheese are a savory and satisfying dish that can be served as a main course for a vegetarian meal or as a delicious appetizer. The combination of hearty portobello mushrooms, creamy cheese filling, and nutritious spinach makes it a flavorful option for any occasion. Enjoy these delicious stuffed mushrooms!

Lemon Garlic Roasted Broccoli

Ingredients:

- 1 lb (450g) broccoli florets
- 2 tablespoons olive oil
- 3 cloves garlic, minced
- Zest of 1 lemon
- 1-2 tablespoons fresh lemon juice (adjust to taste)
- Salt and pepper, to taste
- Grated Parmesan cheese (optional, for serving)

Instructions:

1. **Preheat the Oven:**
    - Preheat your oven to 425°F (220°C).
2. **Prepare the Broccoli:**
    - Cut the broccoli into florets of similar size. If using larger florets, you may want to slice them in half for more even roasting.
3. **Make the Lemon Garlic Mixture:**
    - In a small bowl, combine olive oil, minced garlic, lemon zest, and fresh lemon juice. Stir well to mix.
4. **Coat the Broccoli:**
    - Place the broccoli florets on a large baking sheet. Drizzle the lemon garlic mixture over the broccoli. Use your hands or a spatula to toss the broccoli until evenly coated with the mixture.
5. **Season and Roast:**
    - Spread the broccoli out in a single layer on the baking sheet. Season with salt and pepper to taste.
6. **Roast in the Oven:**
    - Roast the broccoli in the preheated oven for 20-25 minutes, or until the broccoli is tender and the edges are slightly caramelized, stirring halfway through for even cooking.
7. **Serve:**
    - Remove the roasted broccoli from the oven and transfer to a serving dish.
    - Optionally, sprinkle with grated Parmesan cheese before serving.

Lemon Garlic Roasted Broccoli is a delicious and healthy side dish that pairs well with grilled chicken, fish, or as part of a vegetarian meal. The combination of citrusy lemon, savory garlic, and roasted broccoli creates a flavorful and satisfying dish that everyone will enjoy. Enjoy this simple and nutritious recipe!

Harvest Grain Salad with Citrus Vinaigrette

Ingredients:

For the Salad:

- 1 cup quinoa, rinsed
- 1 cup farro or barley, rinsed
- 1/2 cup wild rice, rinsed
- 1 cup dried cranberries or cherries
- 1/2 cup pecans or walnuts, toasted and chopped
- 1/2 cup fresh parsley, chopped
- 1/4 cup green onions, thinly sliced
- 1/4 cup feta cheese or goat cheese, crumbled (optional)

For the Citrus Vinaigrette:

- 1/4 cup olive oil
- Juice of 1 orange
- Juice of 1 lemon
- Zest of 1 lemon
- 1 tablespoon honey or maple syrup
- 1 tablespoon Dijon mustard
- Salt and pepper, to taste

Instructions:

1. **Prepare the Grains:**
   - In separate pots, cook the quinoa, farro (or barley), and wild rice according to package instructions. Drain any excess water and let them cool to room temperature.
2. **Toast the Nuts:**
   - In a dry skillet over medium heat, toast the pecans or walnuts until fragrant and lightly browned, stirring frequently to prevent burning. Remove from heat and let them cool before chopping.
3. **Make the Citrus Vinaigrette:**
   - In a small bowl or jar, whisk together the olive oil, orange juice, lemon juice, lemon zest, honey or maple syrup, Dijon mustard, salt, and pepper until well combined.
4. **Assemble the Salad:**
   - In a large salad bowl, combine the cooked and cooled quinoa, farro (or barley), and wild rice.
   - Add the dried cranberries (or cherries), toasted and chopped nuts, chopped parsley, and sliced green onions. Toss gently to mix.
5. **Add the Dressing:**

- Drizzle the citrus vinaigrette over the salad ingredients, starting with half of the dressing. Toss well to coat evenly. Add more dressing as needed, tasting as you go.

6. **Garnish and Serve:**
    - If using, sprinkle crumbled feta cheese or goat cheese over the top of the salad.
    - Serve the Harvest Grain Salad immediately, or chill in the refrigerator for a couple of hours to allow the flavors to meld.

Harvest Grain Salad with Citrus Vinaigrette is a versatile dish that can be served as a main course for a light lunch or as a side dish for dinner. It's packed with wholesome grains, nuts, and dried fruits, complemented by the bright and tangy citrus dressing. Enjoy this nutritious and delicious salad!

Sauteed Swiss Chard with Garlic and Lemon

Ingredients:

- 1 bunch Swiss chard
- 2 tablespoons olive oil
- 3 cloves garlic, minced
- Zest and juice of 1 lemon
- Salt and pepper, to taste
- Red pepper flakes (optional, for a bit of heat)

Instructions:

1. **Prepare the Swiss Chard:**
    - Wash the Swiss chard thoroughly under cold water. Trim off any tough stems. Separate the leaves from the stems, and chop them into bite-sized pieces. Keep the stems and leaves separate.
2. **Saute the Stems:**
    - Heat olive oil in a large skillet over medium heat. Add the chopped Swiss chard stems and sauté for 3-4 minutes, or until they begin to soften.
3. **Add Garlic and Swiss Chard Leaves:**
    - Add minced garlic to the skillet and cook for 1-2 minutes, stirring constantly, until fragrant.
    - Gradually add the Swiss chard leaves to the skillet, a handful at a time. Cook, stirring frequently, until the leaves are wilted and tender, about 5-7 minutes.
4. **Season with Lemon, Salt, and Pepper:**
    - Stir in the lemon zest and lemon juice. Season with salt, pepper, and red pepper flakes (if using), adjusting to taste.
5. **Serve:**
    - Remove from heat and transfer the sautéed Swiss chard to a serving dish.
    - Serve immediately as a nutritious side dish or as a bed for grilled chicken, fish, or tofu.

Sauteed Swiss Chard with Garlic and Lemon is a healthy and vibrant dish that pairs well with a variety of main courses. The combination of garlic and lemon enhances the natural flavors of the Swiss chard, making it a delightful addition to any meal. Enjoy this simple and nutritious recipe!

Cauliflower Steaks with Chimichurri Sauce

Ingredients:

For the Cauliflower Steaks:

- 1 large head of cauliflower
- 2-3 tablespoons olive oil
- Salt and pepper, to taste

For the Chimichurri Sauce:

- 1 cup fresh parsley, finely chopped
- 1/4 cup fresh cilantro, finely chopped
- 3 cloves garlic, minced
- 1 shallot, finely chopped (optional)
- 1/4 cup red wine vinegar
- 1/2 cup olive oil
- Juice of 1 lemon
- 1/2 teaspoon red pepper flakes (adjust to taste)
- Salt and pepper, to taste

Instructions:

1. **Prepare the Cauliflower Steaks:**
    - Preheat your oven to 400°F (200°C).
    - Remove the leaves from the cauliflower and trim the stem end so it sits flat on the cutting board.
    - Carefully slice the cauliflower into 1-inch thick steaks. You should get about 2-3 steaks from one large head of cauliflower, depending on its size.
    - Place the cauliflower steaks on a baking sheet lined with parchment paper. Brush both sides of each steak with olive oil and season with salt and pepper.
2. **Roast the Cauliflower Steaks:**
    - Roast the cauliflower steaks in the preheated oven for 25-30 minutes, flipping halfway through, until they are tender and golden brown on the edges.
3. **Make the Chimichurri Sauce:**
    - While the cauliflower steaks are roasting, prepare the chimichurri sauce. In a medium bowl, combine the finely chopped parsley, cilantro, minced garlic, shallot (if using), red wine vinegar, olive oil, lemon juice, red pepper flakes, salt, and pepper. Mix well to combine.
4. **Serve:**
    - Once the cauliflower steaks are done roasting, transfer them to serving plates.
    - Spoon a generous amount of chimichurri sauce over each cauliflower steak.
    - Garnish with additional chopped herbs or a drizzle of olive oil, if desired.
    - Serve the cauliflower steaks with chimichurri sauce immediately while warm.

Cauliflower Steaks with Chimichurri Sauce are a delicious and satisfying vegetarian dish that can be served as a main course or a hearty side. The tangy and herbaceous chimichurri sauce complements the roasted cauliflower steaks perfectly, making it a flavorful addition to your meal. Enjoy this nutritious and flavorful recipe!

Asparagus and Gruyere Tart

Ingredients:

For the Tart Shell:

- 1 sheet of puff pastry, thawed if frozen
- Flour, for dusting

For the Filling:

- 1 bunch of asparagus spears (about 1 lb), tough ends trimmed
- 1 cup shredded Gruyere cheese
- 1/2 cup grated Parmesan cheese
- 2 tablespoons olive oil
- 2 cloves garlic, minced
- Salt and pepper, to taste
- Fresh thyme leaves (optional, for garnish)

Instructions:

1. **Preheat the Oven:**
    - Preheat your oven to 400°F (200°C).
2. **Prepare the Tart Shell:**
    - Lightly flour a work surface and roll out the puff pastry into a rectangle large enough to fit your baking sheet or tart pan. Transfer the rolled-out pastry to a baking sheet lined with parchment paper.
3. **Prepare the Asparagus:**
    - In a medium bowl, toss the trimmed asparagus spears with olive oil, minced garlic, salt, and pepper.
4. **Assemble the Tart:**
    - Sprinkle the shredded Gruyere cheese and grated Parmesan cheese evenly over the puff pastry, leaving a border around the edges.
5. **Arrange the Asparagus:**
    - Arrange the seasoned asparagus spears in a single layer over the cheese, slightly overlapping if needed.
6. **Bake the Tart:**
    - Bake the tart in the preheated oven for 20-25 minutes, or until the pastry is golden brown and the asparagus is tender.
7. **Serve:**
    - Remove the tart from the oven and let it cool slightly on a wire rack.
    - Garnish with fresh thyme leaves, if using.
    - Slice and serve the Asparagus and Gruyere Tart warm or at room temperature.

This Asparagus and Gruyere Tart makes a wonderful appetizer or a light main course served with a side salad. The combination of tender asparagus and creamy Gruyere cheese on a flaky puff pastry crust creates a flavorful and elegant dish that's perfect for any occasion. Enjoy this delicious tart!

Sweet Potato and Black Bean Enchiladas

Ingredients:

- 2 medium sweet potatoes, peeled and diced into small cubes
- 1 can (15 oz) black beans, drained and rinsed
- 1 small onion, diced
- 2 cloves garlic, minced
- 1 teaspoon ground cumin
- 1 teaspoon chili powder
- Salt and pepper, to taste
- 2 cups enchilada sauce (store-bought or homemade)
- 8-10 corn tortillas
- 1 cup shredded cheese (cheddar, Monterey Jack, or a blend)
- Chopped cilantro, for garnish (optional)
- Sour cream or Greek yogurt, for serving (optional)

Instructions:

1. **Preheat Oven and Prepare Sweet Potatoes:**
     - Preheat your oven to 400°F (200°C). Place the diced sweet potatoes on a baking sheet lined with parchment paper. Drizzle with olive oil, season with salt and pepper, and toss to coat evenly. Roast in the preheated oven for 20-25 minutes or until tender and lightly browned, stirring halfway through.
2. **Prepare Filling:**
     - In a skillet, heat a bit of olive oil over medium heat. Add the diced onion and cook until softened, about 5 minutes. Add the minced garlic, ground cumin, and chili powder. Cook for another minute until fragrant.
     - Add the black beans and roasted sweet potatoes to the skillet. Stir everything together gently until well combined. Season with salt and pepper to taste. Remove from heat.
3. **Assemble Enchiladas:**
     - Spread a thin layer of enchilada sauce on the bottom of a baking dish.
     - Warm the corn tortillas (you can do this briefly in a microwave or in a skillet) to make them pliable. Spoon some of the sweet potato and black bean filling into each tortilla, roll them up, and place them seam-side down in the baking dish.
4. **Bake:**
     - Once all enchiladas are assembled in the baking dish, pour the remaining enchilada sauce over the top, covering them evenly. Sprinkle shredded cheese on top.
5. **Final Baking:**
     - Cover the baking dish with foil and bake in the preheated oven for 20 minutes. Remove the foil and bake for an additional 5-10 minutes, until the enchiladas are heated through and the cheese is melted and bubbly.

6. **Serve:**
    - Garnish with chopped cilantro if desired. Serve hot with sour cream or Greek yogurt on the side.

Enjoy your Sweet Potato and Black Bean Enchiladas as a flavorful and satisfying meal!

Grilled Eggplant with Tahini Sauce

Ingredients:

- 2 medium-sized eggplants
- Olive oil, for brushing
- Salt and pepper, to taste

For the Tahini Sauce:

- 1/2 cup tahini (sesame seed paste)
- 1/4 cup water (more as needed for desired consistency)
- 2 tablespoons lemon juice
- 1 clove garlic, minced
- 1/2 teaspoon ground cumin
- Salt, to taste
- Chopped fresh parsley or cilantro, for garnish (optional)

Instructions:

1. **Prepare the Eggplant:**
   - Slice the eggplants into rounds, about 1/2 inch thick. You can also slice them lengthwise into planks if preferred.
   - Brush both sides of the eggplant slices with olive oil and season with salt and pepper.
2. **Grill the Eggplant:**
   - Preheat your grill to medium-high heat. Place the eggplant slices on the grill and cook for about 4-5 minutes per side, or until tender and grill marks appear. Cooking time may vary depending on the thickness of your slices and the heat of your grill.
3. **Make the Tahini Sauce:**
   - In a small bowl, whisk together the tahini, water, lemon juice, minced garlic, ground cumin, and salt. Start with 1/4 cup of water and add more gradually until you reach your desired consistency. The sauce should be smooth and creamy.
4. **Assemble and Serve:**
   - Arrange the grilled eggplant slices on a serving platter. Drizzle the tahini sauce generously over the eggplant slices.
   - Garnish with chopped fresh parsley or cilantro if desired.
5. **Enjoy:**
   - Serve the Grilled Eggplant with Tahini Sauce warm or at room temperature. It makes a delicious appetizer, side dish, or even a light main course when served with a side salad or some crusty bread.

This dish is not only flavorful and satisfying but also showcases the wonderful combination of grilled vegetables and creamy tahini sauce. Enjoy!

Beet and Goat Cheese Tartlets

Ingredients:

- 1 sheet of puff pastry, thawed if frozen
- 2-3 medium-sized beets, cooked and thinly sliced (you can roast or boil them until tender)
- 4 oz (about 113g) goat cheese, crumbled
- 1 tablespoon honey
- Fresh thyme leaves (optional, for garnish)
- Salt and pepper, to taste
- Olive oil, for drizzling

Instructions:

1. **Preheat Oven and Prepare Puff Pastry:**
    - Preheat your oven to 400°F (200°C). Line a baking sheet with parchment paper.
    - Roll out the puff pastry sheet on a lightly floured surface. Using a cookie cutter or a small bowl, cut out circles (about 3-4 inches in diameter) from the puff pastry sheet.
2. **Assemble the Tartlets:**
    - Place the puff pastry circles on the prepared baking sheet. Using a fork, prick the centers of the pastry circles to prevent them from puffing up too much during baking.
    - Arrange a few slices of cooked beet on each puff pastry circle. Leave a small border around the edges.
    - Crumble some goat cheese over the beet slices. Drizzle a little honey over each tartlet. Season with salt and pepper to taste.
3. **Bake:**
    - Bake the tartlets in the preheated oven for 15-18 minutes, or until the puff pastry is golden brown and cooked through.
4. **Serve:**
    - Remove the tartlets from the oven and let them cool slightly on a wire rack.
    - Before serving, drizzle a little olive oil over each tartlet and garnish with fresh thyme leaves if desired.
5. **Enjoy:**
    - Serve the Beet and Goat Cheese Tartlets warm as an appetizer or a light meal. They can also be served at room temperature.

These tartlets are not only visually appealing but also pack a delightful combination of flavors that will impress your guests or make for a special treat at home. Enjoy the sweetness of the beets paired with the creamy goat cheese in each bite!

Parsnip and Apple Soup

Ingredients:

- 2 tablespoons unsalted butter or olive oil
- 1 medium onion, chopped
- 3 cloves garlic, minced
- 1 lb (about 450g) parsnips, peeled and chopped (about 4-5 medium parsnips)
- 2 medium apples, peeled, cored, and chopped (use sweet varieties like Gala or Fuji)
- 4 cups vegetable or chicken broth
- 1 teaspoon dried thyme (or 1 tablespoon fresh thyme leaves)
- Salt and pepper, to taste
- 1/2 cup heavy cream (optional, for a creamier soup)
- Chopped fresh parsley or chives, for garnish (optional)
- Croutons or toasted bread, for serving (optional)

Instructions:

1. **Saute the Aromatics:**
   - In a large pot or Dutch oven, melt the butter over medium heat. Add the chopped onion and sauté for 5-6 minutes until softened and translucent.
   - Add the minced garlic and cook for another 1-2 minutes until fragrant.
2. **Cook the Parsnips and Apples:**
   - Add the chopped parsnips and apples to the pot. Stir and cook for about 5 minutes, allowing the flavors to meld together.
3. **Simmer:**
   - Pour in the vegetable or chicken broth to cover the vegetables and fruits. Add the dried thyme (if using fresh thyme, you can add it later). Bring the mixture to a boil, then reduce the heat to low. Cover the pot and let it simmer for about 20-25 minutes, or until the parsnips and apples are tender.
4. **Blend the Soup:**
   - Remove the pot from the heat. Using an immersion blender, blend the soup until smooth and creamy. If you don't have an immersion blender, carefully transfer the soup in batches to a blender and blend until smooth. Be cautious when blending hot liquids.
5. **Season and Finish:**
   - Return the blended soup to the pot if using a blender. Stir in the heavy cream (if using) to add richness to the soup. Season with salt and pepper to taste. If using fresh thyme, add it now and stir.
6. **Serve:**
   - Ladle the soup into bowls. Garnish with chopped fresh parsley or chives if desired. Serve hot, with croutons or toasted bread on the side if you like.

This Parsnip and Apple Soup is perfect for colder days or as a starter for a cozy meal. The combination of parsnips and apples creates a unique flavor profile that is both comforting and satisfying. Enjoy!

Cherry Tomato and Basil Bruschetta

Ingredients:

- 1 pint (about 2 cups) cherry tomatoes, halved
- 1-2 cloves garlic, minced
- 1/4 cup fresh basil leaves, thinly sliced (chiffonade)
- 2 tablespoons extra virgin olive oil
- 1 tablespoon balsamic vinegar (optional)
- Salt and freshly ground black pepper, to taste
- 1 baguette or crusty Italian bread, sliced
- Olive oil, for brushing the bread

Instructions:

1. **Prepare the Tomato Basil Mixture:**
   - In a bowl, combine the cherry tomatoes (halved), minced garlic, and thinly sliced basil leaves.
   - Drizzle the extra virgin olive oil over the mixture. If using, add the balsamic vinegar as well.
   - Season with salt and freshly ground black pepper to taste. Toss gently to combine all the ingredients. Let the mixture sit at room temperature for about 15-20 minutes to allow the flavors to meld together.
2. **Prepare the Bread:**
   - Preheat your grill, grill pan, or oven broiler.
   - Slice the baguette or Italian bread into 1/2-inch thick slices. Brush both sides lightly with olive oil.
3. **Grill or Toast the Bread:**
   - If using a grill or grill pan: Grill the bread slices for about 1-2 minutes on each side, or until they are lightly toasted and have grill marks.
   - If using an oven broiler: Place the bread slices on a baking sheet and broil for about 1-2 minutes on each side, or until they are golden brown and crispy.
4. **Assemble the Bruschetta:**
   - Arrange the toasted bread slices on a serving platter or tray.
   - Spoon the tomato basil mixture generously over each slice of bread, ensuring each piece gets a good amount of tomatoes and basil.
5. **Serve:**
   - Serve the Cherry Tomato and Basil Bruschetta immediately, while the bread is still warm and crispy. Enjoy as a delightful appetizer or a light snack!

This dish is perfect for summer gatherings or any time you want to savor the flavors of fresh tomatoes and basil on crispy bread. It's simple to prepare yet full of vibrant Mediterranean flavors.

Spinach and Ricotta Stuffed Shells

Ingredients:

- 1 box (12-16 oz) jumbo pasta shells
- 1 tablespoon olive oil
- 1 small onion, finely chopped
- 3 cloves garlic, minced
- 5 oz (about 5 cups) fresh spinach, chopped
- 15 oz (about 1 3/4 cups) ricotta cheese
- 1 cup shredded mozzarella cheese, divided
- 1/2 cup grated Parmesan cheese, divided
- 1 egg, lightly beaten
- 1 teaspoon dried oregano
- 1 teaspoon dried basil
- Salt and pepper, to taste
- 24 oz jar of your favorite marinara sauce (or homemade marinara sauce)

Instructions:

1. **Cook the Pasta Shells:**
   - Cook the jumbo pasta shells according to the package instructions until al dente. Drain and set aside to cool slightly.
2. **Prepare the Filling:**
   - Preheat your oven to 350°F (175°C).
   - In a large skillet, heat olive oil over medium heat. Add the chopped onion and cook until softened, about 5-6 minutes.
   - Add the minced garlic and cook for another 1-2 minutes until fragrant.
   - Add the chopped spinach to the skillet and cook until wilted, stirring frequently. This should take about 2-3 minutes. Remove from heat and let cool slightly.
3. **Make the Ricotta Mixture:**
   - In a large bowl, combine the ricotta cheese, 1/2 cup of shredded mozzarella cheese, 1/4 cup of grated Parmesan cheese, beaten egg, dried oregano, dried basil, salt, and pepper.
   - Add the cooked spinach mixture to the bowl and stir until well combined.
4. **Assemble the Stuffed Shells:**
   - Spread about 1/3 of the marinara sauce evenly over the bottom of a 9x13-inch baking dish.
   - Spoon the spinach and ricotta mixture into the cooked pasta shells, filling each shell generously. Place each filled shell into the baking dish on top of the marinara sauce.
5. **Bake:**
   - Pour the remaining marinara sauce over the stuffed shells, covering them evenly.

        - Sprinkle the remaining 1/2 cup of shredded mozzarella cheese and 1/4 cup of grated Parmesan cheese over the top.
        - Cover the baking dish with aluminum foil and bake in the preheated oven for 25 minutes.
6. **Serve:**
        - Remove the foil and bake uncovered for an additional 10 minutes, or until the cheese is melted and bubbly.
        - Remove from the oven and let the stuffed shells cool for a few minutes before serving.
        - Garnish with fresh basil or parsley if desired, and enjoy your Spinach and Ricotta Stuffed Shells warm!

This dish is perfect for a family dinner or a gathering with friends. It's hearty, flavorful, and sure to be a hit at the table!

Roasted Garlic Mashed Potatoes

Ingredients:

- 2 lbs (about 900g) potatoes, such as Russet or Yukon Gold, peeled and cut into chunks
- 1 whole head of garlic
- Olive oil
- 1/2 cup milk (or half-and-half for a richer version)
- 4 tablespoons unsalted butter
- Salt and pepper, to taste
- Chopped fresh chives or parsley, for garnish (optional)

Instructions:

1. **Roast the Garlic:**
    - Preheat your oven to 400°F (200°C).
    - Cut off the top of the whole head of garlic to expose the cloves inside.
    - Place the garlic head on a piece of foil, drizzle with olive oil, and wrap it tightly in the foil.
    - Roast in the preheated oven for about 30-35 minutes, or until the garlic cloves are soft and golden brown. Let it cool slightly.
2. **Cook the Potatoes:**
    - While the garlic is roasting, place the peeled and chopped potatoes in a large pot. Add enough cold water to cover the potatoes by about an inch.
    - Bring the water to a boil over medium-high heat. Reduce the heat to medium-low and simmer the potatoes until tender, about 15-20 minutes.
3. **Prepare the Mashed Potatoes:**
    - Drain the cooked potatoes and return them to the pot.
    - Add the butter to the potatoes and mash them using a potato masher until smooth and creamy.
    - Squeeze the roasted garlic cloves out of their skins directly into the mashed potatoes. Mash them into the potatoes until well combined and smooth.
4. **Add Milk and Seasoning:**
    - Gradually add the milk (or half-and-half) to the mashed potatoes, stirring until you reach your desired creamy consistency.
    - Season with salt and pepper to taste. Adjust the amount of butter or milk as needed to achieve the desired texture.
5. **Serve:**
    - Transfer the roasted garlic mashed potatoes to a serving bowl. Garnish with chopped fresh chives or parsley if desired.
    - Serve hot as a side dish with your favorite main course.

These roasted garlic mashed potatoes are creamy, flavorful, and perfect for any occasion, from weeknight dinners to holiday feasts. The roasted garlic adds a delicious depth of flavor that pairs wonderfully with the creamy potatoes. Enjoy!

Herbed Farro Salad with Roasted Vegetables

Ingredients:

- 1 cup farro
- 2 cups water or vegetable broth
- 1 medium sweet potato, peeled and diced
- 1 medium zucchini, diced
- 1 red bell pepper, diced
- 1 red onion, thinly sliced
- 2 tablespoons olive oil
- Salt and pepper, to taste
- 1/4 cup fresh parsley, chopped
- 2 tablespoons fresh basil, chopped
- 2 tablespoons fresh mint, chopped
- Juice of 1 lemon
- 2 tablespoons balsamic vinegar
- 1/4 cup crumbled feta cheese (optional)
- 1/4 cup toasted pine nuts or chopped walnuts (optional)

Instructions:

1. **Prepare Farro:**
   - Rinse the farro under cold water. In a medium saucepan, bring 2 cups of water or vegetable broth to a boil.
   - Add the rinsed farro to the boiling water. Reduce heat to low, cover, and simmer for 20-25 minutes, or until the farro is tender but still chewy. Drain any excess liquid and let the farro cool slightly.
2. **Roast the Vegetables:**
   - Preheat your oven to 400°F (200°C).
   - On a large baking sheet, toss the diced sweet potato, zucchini, red bell pepper, and thinly sliced red onion with olive oil, salt, and pepper.
   - Spread the vegetables out in a single layer on the baking sheet. Roast in the preheated oven for 20-25 minutes, or until the vegetables are tender and lightly browned. Stir halfway through cooking.
3. **Assemble the Salad:**
   - In a large bowl, combine the cooked farro and roasted vegetables.
   - Add the chopped fresh parsley, basil, and mint to the bowl. Toss gently to combine.
4. **Make the Dressing:**
   - In a small bowl, whisk together the lemon juice, balsamic vinegar, and a tablespoon of olive oil. Season with salt and pepper to taste.
5. **Combine and Serve:**

- Pour the dressing over the farro and roasted vegetable mixture. Toss well to coat everything evenly.
- If using, sprinkle crumbled feta cheese and toasted pine nuts or chopped walnuts over the salad.
- Serve the Herbed Farro Salad with Roasted Vegetables at room temperature or chilled. It can be enjoyed as a main dish or a hearty side.

This salad is packed with nutritious ingredients and bursts with fresh flavors from the herbs and roasted vegetables. It's versatile enough for a weekday lunch or as a colorful addition to any gathering or potluck. Enjoy!

Baked Acorn Squash with Brown Sugar and Cinnamon

Ingredients:

- 2 acorn squash
- 2 tablespoons unsalted butter, melted
- 2 tablespoons brown sugar (more or less to taste)
- 1/2 teaspoon ground cinnamon
- Pinch of salt
- Optional: Maple syrup or honey for drizzling

Instructions:

1. **Preheat the Oven:**
   - Preheat your oven to 400°F (200°C).
2. **Prepare the Acorn Squash:**
   - Wash the acorn squash and pat dry. Slice each squash in half horizontally and scoop out the seeds and stringy pulp with a spoon. Discard the seeds or save them for roasting if desired.
3. **Season the Squash:**
   - Place the squash halves cut-side up on a baking sheet lined with parchment paper.
   - Brush the melted butter evenly over the flesh of each squash half.
   - In a small bowl, mix together the brown sugar, ground cinnamon, and a pinch of salt. Sprinkle this mixture evenly over each squash half.
4. **Bake the Squash:**
   - Bake in the preheated oven for 45-55 minutes, or until the squash is tender when pierced with a fork and the edges are golden brown.
5. **Serve:**
   - Remove the baked acorn squash halves from the oven and let them cool slightly.
   - Optionally, drizzle with maple syrup or honey for extra sweetness.
   - Serve warm as a side dish. The flesh can be scooped out and eaten directly from the skin or cut into wedges.

This Baked Acorn Squash with Brown Sugar and Cinnamon is perfect for fall and winter meals, offering a comforting blend of sweet and savory flavors. It pairs well with roasted meats or as a vegetarian main dish alongside a salad. Enjoy the warm, tender squash with its caramelized edges!

Cabbage Rolls with Tomato Sauce

Ingredients:

For the Cabbage Rolls:

- 1 large head of cabbage (green or Savoy)
- 1 lb (450g) ground meat (beef, pork, or a combination)
- 1 cup cooked rice (white or brown)
- 1 small onion, finely chopped
- 2 cloves garlic, minced
- 1 egg, lightly beaten
- 1/4 cup milk
- 1 teaspoon dried oregano
- 1 teaspoon dried basil
- Salt and pepper, to taste

For the Tomato Sauce:

- 1 can (15 oz) tomato sauce
- 1 can (14.5 oz) diced tomatoes
- 2 tablespoons tomato paste
- 1 small onion, finely chopped
- 2 cloves garlic, minced
- 1 teaspoon dried oregano
- 1 teaspoon dried basil
- Salt and pepper, to taste

Optional Garnish:

- Chopped fresh parsley or dill

Instructions:

1. **Prepare the Cabbage:**
   - Bring a large pot of water to a boil. Carefully remove any damaged outer leaves from the cabbage.
   - Place the whole cabbage head into the boiling water. Cover and cook for about 5-7 minutes, or until the outer leaves are tender and can be easily peeled away from the head.
   - Remove the cabbage from the water and carefully peel off as many large leaves as you can without tearing them. Return the remaining cabbage to the pot and continue boiling if needed to soften more leaves. Set aside the leaves to cool.
2. **Make the Filling:**

- In a large bowl, combine the ground meat, cooked rice, chopped onion, minced garlic, beaten egg, milk, dried oregano, dried basil, salt, and pepper. Mix until well combined.

3. **Assemble the Cabbage Rolls:**
    - Preheat your oven to 350°F (175°C).
    - Place a cabbage leaf on a flat surface. Depending on the size of the leaf, spoon about 1-2 tablespoons of the meat and rice filling onto the center of the leaf.
    - Fold the sides of the leaf over the filling, then roll it up tightly to form a cabbage roll. Repeat with the remaining cabbage leaves and filling.

4. **Prepare the Tomato Sauce:**
    - In a medium saucepan, combine the tomato sauce, diced tomatoes (with their juice), tomato paste, chopped onion, minced garlic, dried oregano, dried basil, salt, and pepper.
    - Bring the sauce to a simmer over medium heat, then reduce the heat and let it simmer gently for about 10-15 minutes, stirring occasionally.

5. **Bake the Cabbage Rolls:**
    - Pour a thin layer of the tomato sauce into the bottom of a large baking dish.
    - Arrange the cabbage rolls seam-side down in the baking dish.
    - Pour the remaining tomato sauce over the cabbage rolls, covering them evenly.

6. **Bake:**
    - Cover the baking dish with foil and bake in the preheated oven for 45-60 minutes, or until the cabbage rolls are cooked through and tender.

7. **Serve:**
    - Remove the foil from the baking dish and let the cabbage rolls cool slightly before serving.
    - Garnish with chopped fresh parsley or dill if desired.
    - Serve the cabbage rolls with a generous spoonful of the tomato sauce. They pair well with crusty bread or mashed potatoes.

This dish is hearty, comforting, and full of flavor. The tender cabbage rolls filled with a savory meat and rice mixture, topped with a rich tomato sauce, make for a satisfying meal that's perfect for sharing with family and friends. Enjoy your homemade Cabbage Rolls with Tomato Sauce!

Grilled Portobello Mushroom Burgers

Ingredients:

- 4 large portobello mushrooms, stems removed
- 2 tablespoons balsamic vinegar
- 2 tablespoons soy sauce or tamari
- 2 tablespoons olive oil
- 2 cloves garlic, minced
- 1 teaspoon dried oregano
- 1 teaspoon dried basil
- Salt and pepper, to taste
- 4 burger buns
- Toppings of your choice (lettuce, tomato, onion, cheese, avocado, etc.)

Instructions:

1. **Marinate the Portobello Mushrooms:**
   - In a shallow dish or a large resealable plastic bag, combine the balsamic vinegar, soy sauce or tamari, olive oil, minced garlic, dried oregano, dried basil, salt, and pepper.
   - Place the portobello mushrooms in the marinade, turning them to coat evenly. Let them marinate for at least 30 minutes, turning occasionally to ensure even marination.
2. **Preheat the Grill:**
   - Preheat your grill or grill pan over medium-high heat. Lightly oil the grill grates to prevent sticking.
3. **Grill the Portobello Mushrooms:**
   - Remove the mushrooms from the marinade, shaking off any excess. Reserve the marinade for basting.
   - Grill the mushrooms for about 4-5 minutes per side, or until they are tender and grill marks appear. Baste with the reserved marinade occasionally during grilling.
4. **Toast the Burger Buns:**
   - While the mushrooms are grilling, lightly toast the burger buns on the grill until they are warmed and slightly crisp.
5. **Assemble the Burgers:**
   - Place each grilled portobello mushroom on a toasted burger bun.
   - Add your favorite toppings such as lettuce, tomato slices, onion slices, cheese, avocado slices, or any other toppings you prefer.
6. **Serve:**
   - Serve the Grilled Portobello Mushroom Burgers immediately, while they are warm and the toppings are fresh.

These grilled portobello mushroom burgers are not only delicious and satisfying but also a healthier alternative to traditional beef burgers. They're packed with umami flavor from the mushrooms and the marinade, making them a crowd-pleaser even among meat-eaters. Enjoy your vegetarian barbecue with these flavorful burgers!

Spring Pea Risotto

Ingredients:

- 1 cup Arborio rice
- 4 cups vegetable or chicken broth (keep warm)
- 1 cup fresh or frozen peas
- 1/2 cup finely chopped onion
- 2 cloves garlic, minced
- 1/2 cup dry white wine
- 1/4 cup grated Parmesan cheese
- 2 tablespoons unsalted butter
- 1 tablespoon olive oil
- 1 tablespoon chopped fresh mint or basil (optional)
- Salt and pepper, to taste
- Lemon zest, for garnish (optional)

Instructions:

1. **Prepare the Peas:**
   - If using fresh peas, blanch them in boiling water for 2-3 minutes, then drain and set aside. If using frozen peas, thaw them according to package instructions.
2. **Cook the Risotto:**
   - In a large saucepan or Dutch oven, heat the olive oil and 1 tablespoon of butter over medium heat.
   - Add the chopped onion and cook for 3-4 minutes until softened.
   - Add the minced garlic and cook for another 1-2 minutes until fragrant.
3. **Toast the Rice:**
   - Add the Arborio rice to the pan and stir to coat it with the oil and butter. Cook for about 2 minutes, stirring frequently, until the rice becomes translucent around the edges.
4. **Deglaze with Wine:**
   - Pour in the white wine and cook, stirring constantly, until the wine has been absorbed by the rice.
5. **Add Broth:**
   - Add the warm broth to the rice mixture, one ladleful at a time, stirring frequently. Allow each addition of broth to be absorbed before adding the next ladleful. This process will take about 20-25 minutes. The rice should be creamy and tender with a slight bite (al dente) when done.
6. **Incorporate Peas:**
   - When the risotto is almost done (after about 15-18 minutes of cooking), stir in the peas. If using fresh peas, add them a few minutes earlier to ensure they cook through.
7. **Finish the Risotto:**

- Once the rice is cooked to your liking and has a creamy consistency, stir in the grated Parmesan cheese and remaining tablespoon of butter.
- Season with salt and pepper to taste. Stir in the chopped fresh mint or basil if using.

8. **Serve:**
    - Serve the Spring Pea Risotto immediately, garnished with a sprinkle of lemon zest if desired.
    - Enjoy this creamy and flavorful risotto as a main dish or as a side alongside grilled chicken or fish.

Spring Pea Risotto is a comforting and elegant dish that celebrates the flavors of the season. The creamy rice paired with sweet peas and fresh herbs makes it a perfect dish for a springtime meal.

Watermelon and Feta Salad with Mint

Ingredients:

- 4 cups cubed seedless watermelon
- 1/2 cup crumbled feta cheese
- 1/4 cup fresh mint leaves, thinly sliced or chopped
- 1 tablespoon extra virgin olive oil
- 1 tablespoon balsamic vinegar or balsamic glaze
- Salt and freshly ground black pepper, to taste

Instructions:

1. **Prepare the Ingredients:**
   - Cut the watermelon into bite-sized cubes if not already done. Remove any seeds if necessary.
   - Crumble the feta cheese into small pieces.
   - Thinly slice or chop the fresh mint leaves.
2. **Assemble the Salad:**
   - In a large bowl, combine the cubed watermelon, crumbled feta cheese, and chopped fresh mint leaves.
3. **Dress the Salad:**
   - Drizzle the extra virgin olive oil and balsamic vinegar (or balsamic glaze) over the salad.
   - Gently toss the salad ingredients together until evenly coated with the dressing.
   - Season with salt and freshly ground black pepper to taste. Remember that feta cheese is salty, so adjust the salt accordingly.
4. **Serve:**
   - Transfer the Watermelon and Feta Salad with Mint to a serving dish or individual plates.
   - Garnish with a few extra mint leaves on top for presentation if desired.
5. **Enjoy:**
   - Serve the salad immediately as a refreshing side dish or a light and healthy appetizer.

Tips:

- **Variations:** You can add additional ingredients like cucumber slices, cherry tomatoes, or red onion slices for more texture and flavor.
- **Make-Ahead:** If preparing ahead of time, keep the salad ingredients separate until ready to serve to maintain freshness and crunch.
- **Storage:** This salad is best enjoyed fresh but can be stored in the refrigerator for a day. The watermelon may release some juice, so drain excess liquid before serving leftovers.

Watermelon and Feta Salad with Mint is perfect for summer gatherings, picnics, or as a colorful addition to any meal. It's a delightful balance of sweet and savory flavors with a refreshing minty twist. Enjoy the burst of flavors in every bite!

Ratatouille Stuffed Peppers

Ingredients:

- 4 bell peppers (any color), tops cut off and seeds removed
- 1 small eggplant, diced into small cubes
- 1 zucchini, diced into small cubes
- 1 yellow squash, diced into small cubes
- 1 red onion, diced
- 2 cloves garlic, minced
- 1 can (14.5 oz) diced tomatoes
- 2 tablespoons tomato paste
- 1 teaspoon dried thyme
- 1 teaspoon dried oregano
- Salt and pepper, to taste
- 2 tablespoons olive oil
- 1/4 cup chopped fresh basil or parsley, plus extra for garnish
- 1/2 cup shredded mozzarella cheese (optional, for topping)

Instructions:

1. **Prepare the Peppers:**
   - Preheat your oven to 375°F (190°C).
   - Cut the tops off the bell peppers and remove the seeds and membranes. Set aside.
2. **Make the Ratatouille Filling:**
   - In a large skillet or frying pan, heat the olive oil over medium heat.
   - Add the diced eggplant, zucchini, yellow squash, and red onion to the skillet. Cook, stirring occasionally, for about 5-7 minutes until the vegetables are slightly softened.
3. **Add Flavor:**
   - Stir in the minced garlic, dried thyme, and dried oregano. Cook for another 1-2 minutes until fragrant.
4. **Combine with Tomatoes:**
   - Add the diced tomatoes and tomato paste to the skillet. Stir well to combine all the ingredients.
   - Season with salt and pepper to taste. Let the mixture simmer for about 10-15 minutes, stirring occasionally, until the vegetables are tender and the flavors have melded together.
5. **Finish the Filling:**
   - Remove the skillet from heat and stir in the chopped fresh basil or parsley. Adjust seasoning if needed.
6. **Stuff the Peppers:**
   - Place the hollowed-out bell peppers upright in a baking dish.

- Spoon the ratatouille filling into each pepper, packing it tightly and filling to the top.

7. **Bake:**
   - Cover the baking dish with foil and bake in the preheated oven for 25-30 minutes, or until the peppers are tender.

8. **Optional: Add Cheese (for topping):**
   - If using shredded mozzarella cheese, remove the foil from the baking dish and sprinkle the cheese over the stuffed peppers.
   - Return the dish to the oven and bake, uncovered, for an additional 5-7 minutes until the cheese is melted and bubbly.

9. **Serve:**
   - Remove the Ratatouille Stuffed Peppers from the oven and let them cool slightly.
   - Garnish with additional chopped fresh basil or parsley if desired.
   - Serve the stuffed peppers warm as a delicious and colorful main dish.

These Ratatouille Stuffed Peppers are packed with flavor from the assortment of vegetables and herbs. They make for a satisfying and nutritious meal that can be enjoyed on its own or paired with a side salad or crusty bread. Enjoy the taste of Provence with this delightful dish!

Corn and Tomato Pie

Ingredients:

- 1 pie crust (store-bought or homemade)
- 3 cups fresh or frozen corn kernels (thawed if using frozen)
- 1 cup cherry tomatoes, halved
- 1/2 cup diced red bell pepper
- 1/2 cup diced onion
- 1 clove garlic, minced
- 1/2 cup mayonnaise
- 1/2 cup shredded cheddar cheese
- 1/2 cup shredded mozzarella cheese
- 1/4 cup grated Parmesan cheese
- 2 tablespoons chopped fresh basil
- 1 tablespoon chopped fresh parsley
- Salt and pepper, to taste

Instructions:

1. **Preheat the Oven:**
   - Preheat your oven to 375°F (190°C). Place the pie crust in a 9-inch pie dish and set aside.
2. **Prepare the Filling:**
   - In a large bowl, combine the corn kernels, cherry tomatoes, diced red bell pepper, diced onion, and minced garlic.
3. **Make the Cheese Mixture:**
   - In a separate bowl, mix together the mayonnaise, shredded cheddar cheese, shredded mozzarella cheese, grated Parmesan cheese, chopped basil, chopped parsley, salt, and pepper.
4. **Combine and Fill the Pie:**
   - Add the cheese mixture to the bowl of vegetables. Stir gently until everything is well combined and evenly coated.
5. **Assemble and Bake:**
   - Spoon the corn and tomato filling into the prepared pie crust, spreading it out evenly.
6. **Bake the Pie:**
   - Place the pie in the preheated oven and bake for 30-35 minutes, or until the filling is bubbly and the crust is golden brown.
7. **Serve:**
   - Remove the Corn and Tomato Pie from the oven and let it cool for a few minutes before slicing.
   - Garnish with additional chopped basil or parsley if desired.
   - Serve warm as a delicious main dish or side dish.

This Corn and Tomato Pie is perfect for summer gatherings or as a comforting meal any time of the year. It's packed with fresh vegetables, creamy cheese, and aromatic herbs, making it a flavorful and satisfying dish for everyone to enjoy.

Roasted Cauliflower with Tahini Yogurt Sauce

Ingredients:

For the Roasted Cauliflower:

- 1 head of cauliflower, cut into florets
- 2-3 tablespoons olive oil
- 1 teaspoon ground cumin
- 1 teaspoon ground paprika
- Salt and pepper, to taste

For the Tahini Yogurt Sauce:

- 1/4 cup tahini
- 1/2 cup plain Greek yogurt
- 2 tablespoons lemon juice
- 1 clove garlic, minced
- 1/2 teaspoon ground cumin
- Salt and pepper, to taste
- Water, as needed to thin the sauce

Optional Garnish:

- Chopped fresh parsley or cilantro
- Toasted pine nuts or sesame seeds

Instructions:

1. **Roast the Cauliflower:**
    - Preheat your oven to 425°F (220°C).
    - In a large bowl, toss the cauliflower florets with olive oil, ground cumin, ground paprika, salt, and pepper until evenly coated.
    - Spread the cauliflower florets in a single layer on a baking sheet lined with parchment paper.
2. **Roast the Cauliflower:**
    - Roast in the preheated oven for 25-30 minutes, or until the cauliflower is tender and caramelized around the edges. Flip the florets halfway through cooking for even roasting.
3. **Make the Tahini Yogurt Sauce:**
    - In a small bowl, whisk together the tahini, Greek yogurt, lemon juice, minced garlic, ground cumin, salt, and pepper until smooth.
    - If the sauce is too thick, add water, a tablespoon at a time, until you reach your desired consistency. The sauce should be creamy and pourable.
4. **Assemble and Serve:**

- Arrange the roasted cauliflower on a serving platter or individual plates.
- Drizzle the tahini yogurt sauce generously over the roasted cauliflower.
- Garnish with chopped fresh parsley or cilantro, and toasted pine nuts or sesame seeds if desired.

5. **Enjoy:**
    - Serve the Roasted Cauliflower with Tahini Yogurt Sauce immediately while still warm.
    - This dish can be served as a flavorful side dish or a light vegetarian main course.

Roasted Cauliflower with Tahini Yogurt Sauce is a delicious and satisfying dish that combines the nuttiness of tahini with the tanginess of yogurt, enhancing the roasted cauliflower beautifully. It's perfect for a healthy dinner or as part of a Mediterranean-inspired meal.

Pumpkin and Sage Pasta

Ingredients:

- 12 oz (340g) pasta of your choice (such as penne, rigatoni, or fettuccine)
- 1 tablespoon olive oil
- 2 tablespoons unsalted butter
- 2 cloves garlic, minced
- 1/4 cup fresh sage leaves, chopped (plus extra for garnish)
- 1 can (15 oz) pumpkin puree
- 1 cup vegetable broth
- 1/2 cup heavy cream
- 1/4 cup grated Parmesan cheese, plus extra for serving
- Salt and pepper, to taste
- Pinch of nutmeg (optional)
- Toasted pine nuts, for garnish (optional)

Instructions:

1. **Cook the Pasta:**
    - Bring a large pot of salted water to a boil. Cook the pasta according to the package instructions until al dente. Reserve about 1 cup of pasta water, then drain the pasta.
2. **Prepare the Pumpkin and Sage Sauce:**
    - In a large skillet or saucepan, heat the olive oil and butter over medium heat until the butter has melted.
    - Add the minced garlic and chopped sage leaves. Cook for about 1 minute until fragrant.
3. **Add Pumpkin Puree:**
    - Stir in the pumpkin puree and vegetable broth. Bring the mixture to a simmer.
4. **Simmer and Season:**
    - Reduce the heat to low. Stir in the heavy cream and grated Parmesan cheese. Season with salt, pepper, and a pinch of nutmeg (if using). Simmer for about 5-7 minutes, stirring occasionally, until the sauce is heated through and slightly thickened.
5. **Combine Pasta and Sauce:**
    - Add the cooked pasta to the skillet with the pumpkin sauce. Toss gently to coat the pasta evenly with the sauce. If the sauce is too thick, add a little reserved pasta water to thin it out.
6. **Serve:**
    - Divide the Pumpkin and Sage Pasta among serving plates or bowls.
    - Garnish with extra chopped sage leaves, grated Parmesan cheese, and toasted pine nuts if desired.
7. **Enjoy:**

- Serve the Pumpkin and Sage Pasta immediately while warm.
- This dish pairs well with a crisp green salad and crusty bread for a complete meal.

Pumpkin and Sage Pasta is a comforting and creamy dish that's perfect for autumn or any time you're craving a hearty pasta dish with a twist. The combination of pumpkin, sage, and Parmesan creates a rich and flavorful sauce that complements the pasta beautifully. Enjoy this delicious meal!

Blueberry Basil Lemonade

Ingredients:

- 1 cup fresh blueberries
- 1/2 cup fresh basil leaves, plus extra for garnish
- 1 cup granulated sugar (adjust to taste)
- 1 cup water
- 1 cup freshly squeezed lemon juice (about 4-6 lemons)
- 4 cups cold water
- Ice cubes

Instructions:

1. **Make Blueberry Basil Simple Syrup:**
    - In a small saucepan, combine the blueberries, basil leaves, granulated sugar, and 1 cup of water.
    - Bring the mixture to a boil over medium-high heat, stirring occasionally to dissolve the sugar.
    - Reduce the heat to low and simmer for about 5-7 minutes, crushing the blueberries with a spoon as they cook.
    - Remove from heat and let the mixture steep for 15-20 minutes to infuse the flavors.
2. **Strain and Cool:**
    - Strain the blueberry basil syrup through a fine-mesh sieve into a bowl, pressing down on the solids to extract as much liquid as possible. Discard the solids.
    - Allow the syrup to cool completely. You can speed up the cooling process by placing it in the refrigerator.
3. **Mix the Lemonade:**
    - In a large pitcher, combine the freshly squeezed lemon juice and 4 cups of cold water.
    - Stir in the cooled blueberry basil syrup. Taste and adjust sweetness by adding more water or sugar if desired.
4. **Serve:**
    - Fill glasses with ice cubes and pour the Blueberry Basil Lemonade over the ice.
    - Garnish each glass with a sprig of fresh basil leaves for an extra touch of freshness and aroma.
5. **Enjoy:**
    - Stir the lemonade before serving to mix any settled ingredients.
    - Serve immediately and enjoy this refreshing Blueberry Basil Lemonade on a hot day or as a delightful drink for any occasion.

This Blueberry Basil Lemonade is not only visually appealing but also bursting with flavors that complement each other beautifully. The combination of blueberries, basil, and lemon creates a refreshing and slightly tangy drink that is sure to be a hit with family and friends.

www.ingramcontent.com/pod-product-compliance
Lightning Source LLC
LaVergne TN
LVHW081612060526
838201LV00054B/2213